POETRY, PROSE

Poetry, Prose and Pondering

Charlotte Richardson

By

Charlotte Richardson

CREMER PRESS

First Published in Great Britain in 2005 by
Charlotte Richardson.
C/O Cremer Press, Blackburn.

ISBN 1 898722 58 7

Printed and Bound by
Edmund Mercer, Cremer Press,
45 Harrison Street, Blackburn. Lancs. BB2 2JE.

CONTENTS ONE

CONTENTS TWO

CONTENTS THREE

CONTENTS FOUR

CONTENTS FIVE

INTRODUCTION

When you are alone, your thoughts tend to flow and stray
To the once upon a time, that made your day.
Memories drip from a niche in your brain,
Growing more revealing, more fluid, like tears in rain.
All part of a sequence, formed in the flow
Of life's journey, a long time ago.
Where I was born, in a little Lancashire town,
I struggled with adversity as others around,
Hoping to hear a Bluebird sing,
Bringing happiness on its wing.
Dreams always dance, and are picked out of the queue
Of heartbreak and sadness, and are magic in lieu
Of all the laughter you missed on the way,
As Nemesis decreed it was his day.
But youth is resilient to a will-o-the-wisp call,
And the world on its axis gives measure to the goal
That someone, somewhere, had a destiny planned,
Where dreams and magic will never be banned.
Acquired through kindness and totally free,
I notched up a friend on my memory tree,
Streaming in sunshine on a cold winter's day,
Rosy vistas blotting out, the colour of grey.
Nostalgic moments in quicksilver light
A beautiful friendship heartfelt and bright.
Precious pieces of time, genuine pearls on a string,
Dripping with love for the memories they bring.

Hope you enjoy reading this book as much as
I enjoyed writing it.

Charlotte Richardson.

A BEAUTIFUL DAY

Butterflies, in colour, bees in flight and drone,
Wild flowers in meadows, in summer haze,
A breeze whispering in rhythm,
Too tired for a stronger faze.
Rippling waters a-sparkle in the warmth of the sun
A luring invite for moments of fun.
To children full of laughter,
Bubbling voices throng,
In games of pretend, in daydreams of youth
Where children belong.
Golden days and blue skies, when the world was new,
When a riot of wild flowers, is fashioned into a bouquet for you.
Birds chirp in chorus, a gentle lark,
A blue-tit, a starling, just a few in the arc
Of those golden days, skies warm and blue,
Would they go on forever, repeat before they're due?
Mellow they pass, into a balmy purple night,
The sun kissing the horizon, a beautiful sight!
Another sunset, another dawn, another round of light,
The darkness lightening to grey,
Streaking fingers of rose, painting the way.
Fanning the gold of the sun, into another beautiful day.

A BIT O' GOSSIP

"Hello there Martha, how've ya bin. It's bin quite sum time thad thy face I've sin. What wi' cleanin', not but I do much o' thad mind. Them day's 'ave gone lass, an' work's easy ta find. It's t' shoppin', an' payin' t' bills, an' a mekin special calls, not to mention folks ya meet in t' street, pickin' neighbours full o' holes. If it weren't fer them, yer wud ged round a treat. An' how sum go on, geddin' fair throng. Yer don't know if tha's comin' or goin', it teks so long.

An' it's all about nowt, when all's sed an' done. Well it meks yer mad, fer wastin' time ain't no fun, when yer've ged ta know nowt, when all's sed an' done.

I was goin' ta ask yer, have yer sin 'yon won' of late? I heard she had bin stoppin' in. It must be something she's ate, fer she always goes out, aye every night. She likes her gin does 'yon one', before sum food onta plate.

Yer heard she'd got what? O is thad all, her she's not used to pain. Now if she had had it like me, she'd be goin' up t' wall. They say everything comes ta them thad wait, well her time is now, an' it's long past sell date.

But it won't stop *him* in, he'll be up an' out. An' he'll sup her share, with no but a doubt. If he were mine, I'd ring his neck, for he has never bin owt, an' she knows it, by heck! Yer know he's had many a bit on ta side, an' now he'll be mekin' up for t' times he did bide.

Well strike me it is Mary Ellen, an' she's comin' this way, an' t' rate she goin' at, it will tek all day. She is fair bad on her feet, but don't turn her way, then she won't twig we've had owt ta say.

An' how 'ave ya bin Mary Ellen, we heard ya'd bin bad, right poorly like, bud yer should tek more care, an' leave more to him, right! Fer like all t' fellas, he'll let thy do and do, an' he'll soon have another when he's buried you.

You're doin' yer best ta manage, well thad's not right. Trust a fella ta dodge shoppin', an' eat as his right. We had bin sayin', Martha an' me, through thee havin' thad pain, we hadn't sin you out, an' we thought it a shame. But it seems thad thy husband, he's all right, was it this week or last he was was wi' thad blonde, t' other night?

Now I am nod sayin' there was owt wrong, an' I just ferged her name. He'd just gone fer drinks, after havin' a game. Bingo tha knows, I can't win a thing. Now what was it she won when she was joinin' wi' him?

Now are yer sure ya can manage, fer I'll be goin' your way, fer I've sed all ta Martha, what I had ta say. Fer when thy lives on thy own, an' thy never goes out, all thy do is brew tay, to while t' time away. Tha hears nowt, and sees nowt, and thinks thad they'll tek yer away.

Then standin' on t' doorstep, thy accidentally hears a bit o' gossip goin' on, amidst laughter and leers. Scandal so thick, thy cud cut it wi' a knife. It fair bucks thee up some, an' puts t' interest back in yer life."

A CENTENARY NIGHT

An old stone bridge, with its blackened wall,
Remote in the shadow of a chimney tall.
A hotchpotch of life, lived on terraces nearby,
Their narrow cobbled streets, pouring smoke in the sky.
Their secrets, intrigues, they try to hide,
Avoiding the gossips, they have to bide.

Proximity swamps the urge, to get up and go,
With zealous moments melting, like flurries of snow.
The mind gets resigned, for this is home,
A welcome harbour, for whoever did roam.
With love and hate blending, in the daily round,
With the growing tolerance, that is easily found
In the monotony of a shared toil,
Often masked in temper, hasty words a foil.

Rebelling at defeat, at fate's tangled weave,
With the challenge to vie, demanding a super heave
To be less obtuse to mundane things,
To life, to truth, to wedding rings.

Now mind and mood are letting go,
And the scene brings fresh thoughts, sure if slow,
As a sliver of moon casts an eerie glow
On a dank drop of canal, with a sluggish flow.

One hears the clatter of clogs mingle, with the clip-clop of a horse,
The whole village now in throng, turning out in force.
With a quick rapport from a local sage,
To undulating voices adding wit and rage.

The cobbles meander along, down under an arch
Past church and mill, people happily march
To a verdant spot, of soft sprung ground,
Where over the verge, a fountain and cross can be found
Spruced for the occasion, with garlands and light
Winking fairy-like colours, into the night.

A hand bell is rung, a speaker calls,
The celebrations are swinging, it's the centenary ball!
The village hall being the pivot, be-flowered, blazing with light,
Transforming the drab, to a festive sight.

The clog dancers now clopping, shiny clogs well into their stride,
Complete with a maypole, be-ribbonned with bells
Children dancing, puffed out with pride
Near a carousel, full and whirling, playing razzmatazz,
Its cocks and hens rotating up and down to the jazz.

A few hours of gaiety, away from the dross,
With the buffet being paid for, by the 'Bigwig' - the boss.
Suspended moments, to collect and store,
To wrap up in nostalgia, away from the core
Of terraces and back streets, away from the world,
Where at six each work morning, the blind is hurriedly unfurled
To answer the knocker-up's rap, on window or door,
The shatterer of dreams, bringing reality once more!

The time for earning a living, to face the cold morning air,
To tramp down a street, probably rain-lashed and bare.
Full of inertia, and too tired to care,
Over the bridge to the gates of the mill,
Where others now walk, sleepy, subdued, their voices still.
Immune to their neighbours, knowing the time is now,
Work being the thing to get on with, and how!
Conscientious concentration, willing the hours away

To a more favourable time, at the end of the day.
When thrust and zeal grinds a slower wheel,
Allowing one to be human, with thoughts near tangible and real.
So real, filling the brain and setting the seal.

A dream had come true,
With an old love made new.
With the music, and the magic, that exuded on sight,
Yes, one quite special, happy centenary night!

A DIFFERENT VIEW

I awoke to birdsong and skies clear blue,
A maple tree swayed, all drenched in dew,
An intruder doing what all birds do.
Rolling meadows in shades of green,
Crazy divisions, stone-wall laced.
One golden barley, the like I had never seen.
It pleasured my eye, its prolific hue
Awaiting the reaper, to do his due.
Lethargic on my comfy bed I lay,
All thoughts in limbo, for the chores of the day.
I inhaled fresh air, with nostrils a-flare,
The moment holding my senses, holding my stare.
Would a cloud appear and break the spell
Of me lying here in my warm bed, who's to tell?
Enjoying the view,
Now the excuse for all I had said I was going to do,
Even if only in my mind,
When the truth is before me
As on awakening I did find.
This country vista, this clear blue sky,
To a 'Towny' so beautiful, that I could cry!
Emotions adrift, I rationalise as I sigh,
Stir myself and think, "Why oh why?
Living here has transformed all, has set me free
To find green fields, and birds that sing in a maple tree.
Simple to you, so wondrous to me,
All my tomorrow's, so different always before me,
I can awake and see,
It's glorious Wales for me!"

A MEMORY FLASH

Parts of my life I have written out in rhyme,
When thoughts have tumbled, and when I felt fine.
Not often these days is the energy flow,
For the years diminish your get up and go.
With reminisce the only portal left,
The spur for pondering to the bereft.
Shafts of moonlight are dancing again,
Indelible the picture, in your brain,
As stalks of barley grass tickle your chin,
Whilst reaching for a poppy, seeded within
That overgrown meadow, where you had happened to stray,
Full of happiness on that summer's day.
A voice calls your name, there's a figure by the stile,
You join him with laughter, full of beguile.
Snatches of memories of times passed by,
When two people were one, in life's reach for the sky.
The sun still shines through my windowpane,
And the tree in my backyard, sings a refrain
Stirred by the wind of happy acclaim
Of a snowdrop's thrust, through a winter's snow,
Elements of life's reminisce and recycled in nature's flow.

A MOMENT IN TIME

How long I had walked, I did not know,
Just an aimless stroll, with an occasional thought,
Reminiscence bringing nostalgia, which I had not sought.
No time check, no motive, no one to say,
"You must hurry home now, better be on your way."
I could fill, or empty my mind at will,
Sit or stand motionless, still
Observing the unfamiliar, stop and enjoy
This pleasant meander, such a revealing ploy,
Where a straddle of trees
Seemed to sweep to the sea.

In depth, a profusion of bark and leaf,
A barrier dark, a natural reef,
Skirting smooth golden sands and rocks of time,
With a rugged beauty, commanding, fine.
Sun and sea, wind and rain,
Adding, and taking, playing nature's game.
A sway of greenery, with an urge to roam,
To burrow roots into the heart of the stone.
Sprouting wayward tendrils from crevice and nook,
Acclaiming the rock to be somehow prone
To softening the bluff, to compensate for the way
The relentless sea pounds night and day.
Hurling its anger in spewing spray,
Or caressing with droplets, giving a natural trace
Of minerals, and compounds, colouring the grey,
Eroded lesions, on its granite face.
This picturesque view pleased my eye,
As perpetual seas swelled, rolling by
As white horses danced on the curling sea,
Swirling this moment in time into memory for me.

With the wind in rhythm, a murmuring sound
Rolling in breakers, hurling froth around
The resilient sands, the cliffs impassive wall,
My eyes sweeping the sea, enjoying it all.
The elegance above, towering pines,
Deeming to salute and dampen a low trailing shrub
That had flowered over all.
Blowing now in unison with that upper crown
Of rustling trees, some evergreen,
Some changing into an autumn gown.
The untrodden sands were left high and dry,
Inviting me to tarry, pause, and wonder why?
So being I remember, so being I sigh,
That half of my life has frittered by
Minus this beauty, and again I ask why
I had never passed this way before?
Taken time off to stand, and see,
Tufts of white cloud in the blue of the sky,
Sail to the horizon, fluid and free.
With nature's colours scattered around,
From sand and rocks, to the high sprung ground.

I thanked God for this moment, and finding it so,
A tranquil spot, where I can come and go,
A place to savour, if but briefly in time,
Which today I have found, making it mine
To cherish and store in my memory book,
And I know you won't mind, if I take one last look!

A NIGHT IN MAY

Down Kensington way one Monday in May,
A drama unfolded at 16 Princess Gate,
Police ringed an Embassy
Terrorised and filled with hate.

Bombs and gunfire, and a smoking pall
Added to the quickening, confusing the overriding gall.
People in there, how did they fare,
Would we ever see them again, would they come out whole?
In body that is, but what of their soul?

Would it bear the scars, and the nightmares till
The heart ceased to beat, till
Mind and body subsided into their last deep sleep.
Who were the men, hooded and crouched on the sill,
Armed and waiting on the balcony, tense and still?

Suddenly activity, police scurrying around,
Handle a stretcher, with a body from the house, through the ground
Hurriedly to an ambulance, as flames and fire residue,
Spew and blacken the walls
Of a portico window, with more acrid smoke palls
Belching high, and growing more strong,
God help them inside, I pray nothing goes wrong

For hostages and gunmen, their time draws near and must bide,
Tension, terror, let good decide
Who waves a white flag, who will get free
To carry on with living, who will it be?

More stretchers are rushed in, more people led out too,
More running figures to the rescue break through
With more water being hosed on the fire's flaming rage,
With more tragedy in that house than would fill this page.

First aid now in play, will providence allow, it is not too late
For the human flotsam, proved to be the bait
For a festering of emotions, stirred with hate,
For what, and for whom, for the answer we'll wait.

As the sun goes down, smoke drifts across Hyde Park,
Nature immune from revenge from the heart.
Immune from heartache, and hope that lights up the dark,
From human frailty, on this scene so stark.

A PIECE OF LIFE

My brother was six years younger than me,
And his needs I had tended from birth you see.
As with the baby, whose age in months was three.
Twelve-years old myself, I washed and scoured floors clean,
Polishing the black-leaded range, till it did glint and gleam.
I played out with friends when time did allow,
Or if a penny I got Saturday, to Empress pictures I would bow
Giving Joe Bradley the proprietor, my penny in his hand,
I skipped down the gangway to the strains of a band.
This band was really an organ, the music manually played
In a box by the stage, where flowers and palms were arrayed
With the words thrown on the screen, a white ball bouncing each one,
As each note was played.
I enjoyed the sing-song before the matinée did start,
Chatting and laughing with a happy childish heart
Waiting eagerly for the picture, and the lights to dim,
To be swept into raptures of a wonderful day,
Of low cut bodies, displayed garters.
Some you thought were a sin.
Handsome cowboys being the pivot, with dance-hall girls in the West,
An American revelation, but we liked the Indians the best.
Mountains and deserts, the screen did unfurl,
Arid and barren under a merciless sun,
Vast and exciting where the hero always won.
This America, we watched with stars in our eyes,
But it could have been outer-space, without any surprise.
For to cross an ocean that rolled, seemed a life span away,
Seemingly impossible fantasy, to us in that day.
Then back to earth, and home for tea,
That was debatable, depending on how things had turned out you see,
For Saturday was the day, during shopping my mother would stray,
Meeting and going with friends on the way

Into the nearest pub for a drink, eventually forgetting the time,
Happy indulgence erasing all thoughts of time,
Whether we had any tea went without reason or rhyme.
But come what may, the hours ticked away
In the nearest pub to the close of day
Creeping on to midnight the human exodus did start
The alcoholic friction, the muddle a part
Of anything or anyone who happened to be there,
Abrasive words, heated tempers, a punch-up would flare.

Our back street was noted for these regular do's,
Packed with natural characters, who whether they did win or lose
Would be back in the 'Lanky' the very next day,
Fretting and boozing, in the regular way.
Escaping the drab daily round,
Passing the time, for people who never got up off the ground.
Victims of circumstance, in a poverty trap,
Who tired of struggling, let fantasy overlap
With a Guinness or beer in their favourite spot,
The 'Lancashire' and 'Yorkshire' and when things got hot,
They gave it all they'd got.
Simply straying out of line
Just trying to stay human, and feeling fine
For with just one more drink, all was rosy this time.

A PLACE TO GO

To get away from material things,
From the human element, and obligations they bring,
To leave tarmacadam roads, and walk soft sprung earth,
See tumbling waters, sparkle from their place of birth
High in a mountain, from an eroding niche,
Gravitating in volume, to a cascading pitch,
To walk profuse leafed woodlands, full of birdsong,
Its silent secrets nurturing creatures, alive and throng.
To glimpse hedgerows thickly pregnant, bursting blossoms in May,
A haven for the cuckoo, purloining nests to survey.
To swivel your eyes towards heaven, so clear, so high,
So full of silence, that you want to cry,
That this is the moment you have willed it to be,
To reminisce in memory, to assess your life,
Touching new horizons, dreams for tomorrow, expectancy rife!

A QUESTION

How do you get used to being alone?
Seeing curtains and furnishings, static, forlorn.
With no one to say, "This room needs a new look!"
With only yourself to plump up a cushion, or pick up a book.
With only one chair which you occupy,
Somehow obtrusive, rather rude
To the solitary air the others exude.
How do you refrain from screaming out loud,
When silence is the only sound?
Yes, how do you cope, come to terms with your lot,
Adapt to a new role, to the perfect union, you once had got.
So full of memories it breaks your heart,
How do you go on and play your part
Facing each day with its waiting routine,
Which gets done if at all, in a half-hearted way.
For with only you to assess, to leave or to clean,
The hours pass by, there is no one coming, no one has been.
How do you stop this reminiscent flow
That creeps with the solitude, and won't let go?
The immediate holds nothing, it is always the past,
With the happiness of years, how the memories last.
They're always there, refreshing as summer rain,
You cherish all the more, as they flow in your brain,
Banishing gloom for a short while,
With a happy sigh and a tight-lipped smile.
Once your life was full, with the family there,
But all married now they have their own life and care.
Your world revolved around them each waking day,
Eagerly doing, and noting all they did say.
Cooking, sewing, not enough hours for your labours of love,
For the family you were blessed with from God up above.

Your giving was a pleasure,
You thought you were lucky just to be you,
And that your family was well, and you had done your due.
It hurt when eventually they all went away,
But it was as inevitable as night and day.
But when your partner goes your world seems to end,
A nameless fear fills your heart, which you struggle to fend.
You are somehow forgotten, in the turning years,
A nonentity left behind, frequently battling with tears.
Bravely smiling at the public at large,
And giving all the right answers to those who barge
In an off-handed way, to probe your plight; they being secure
And sheltered in their own sphere.
Prone to theories, and the occasional jeer.
Having no conception of life alone,
The struggle to see light in the dregs of despair,
Carrying on and trying to show a face of 'don't care'.

So how do you get used to being alone,
The indifference without, and the emptiness zone?
Your quiet room, full of silent sound,
Does a prayer help you, as I have found
How to cope with this new life, which to many is old,
You know you will do so, for you have entered the fold.
Your convictions grow strong, God has heard your prayer,
And with a smile, and a kind word, He will always be there!

A ROYAL DATE
(Written on the expected birth of Prince William)

The year is ending, and Christmas draws near,
And the birth of the Saviour veers thoughts to the New Year,
To the passing of winter, and into spring,
To burst into June, when hearts will surely sing
In this year in time, 1982,
That soon, very soon, another birth is due
That will bring hopes a welling in quite a few.

Royal hearts, with flustered musings so,
That the Princess of Wales will deliver more quick than slow,
For all the world waits, and is having a go,
Speculating and betting, will a girl or boy
Fill the Royal parents with overwhelming joy?
A new Princess or Prince, his heritage a king,
To go down in history, whatever will this birth bring?

A small warm bundle with tiny fingers curled,
Opening unfocused eyes, on a strange new world.
God bless this new babe, born like you and me,
And already burdened down, with destiny.
Long may its childhood be happy and gay,
With no wicked fairy to steal it away.
With no evil force to cast a spell
On this latest arrival of the family loved so well.

A SECOND TIME

Tumbling thoughts, a jumble in my brain,
Pensive, lingering, reverting to singular, the one always the same.
Full of pent-up emotions, subconsciously aware
Of the immediate around, that stripped my soul bare.
A reverie of half forgotten things loomed clear as light,
Suspending the moment, making the day more bright.
Or was it this niche where my footsteps had strayed,
And the longed for nostalgia, on which my conscious had laid?
Where was the boy - did I break his heart?
How did it happen, and why did we have to part?
And what of the years lightly thrown away?
Does only experience quote the price we pay?
These lanes I have walked many times before,
In snow and rain, and mellow as now.
The sun filtering shapes through an oak's swinging bough,
A silver birch, rustling alone,
Seemed a kindred spirit, trying to atone.

With its dancing leaves reaching out to where
Elegant poplars spaced with care,
Sheltered a garden and cottage there.
A sigh escaped me as memories flowed on,
Was I to blame for what was dead and gone?
Jerked out of my musings, footsteps fell on the lane,
He was walking towards me, the cottage to gain.
The wind ruffled my hair as I slipped off the stile,
My heart beating fast, as if I had run a mile.
Not the twilight hour, just the closing of day,
With mutual recognition bringing along
A thousand emotions that smote like a song.
Questions demanding answers, wanting to pour out free,
But something in his eyes silenced me.

"An Indian Summer," I heard him sigh,
Better late than never, prolonged a beautiful sight,
Like the premonition you would come that flared last night.
I plucked a rose and its perfumed heart
Spread the aura, with you a part,
A forever part, wrapped in the reminiscence of this place,
And now this moment in time, we meet face to face.

I never heard the rest, my eyes filled with tears,
Could we ever make up for all the wasted years?
Would happiness flow in two hearts now full,
Blessing the day a revelation had touched them,
Had stirred thoughts to mull,
To pick up the threads of a broken life,
And try again as man and wife.

A SMALL BIT OF IRELAND

A promontory of crags, with lesions deep and warm,
Dipping down to a sea; its wash, soothing and calm.
Hiding its fury, its thrashing spray,
Its floating flotsam, in a casual way.
A honeycomb of stones, higher still,
Form a mosaic pattern, on a turf-covered hill.
Crater like, questionable, remote and strange,
Fashioned from outer-space, disputable the hand that did arrange
Susceptibility on a moonlight night,
Amidst wild flowers, gorse and sea, what might
Conjure music, haunting and sweet,
Imbuing the moment, the memory to keep.
Spells, open to reason,
From locals that be Irish Celts, character and race
Proud of this dingle, with its timeless face.

Crags and inlets running free,
With an ever surging fluid sea.
Misshapen stones midst shingle sand,
Step carefully now, or take my hand,
Till that shard of cloud,
Disperses away, exposing the wild sweeping soft green band
Of undulating grasses, peppered with a silvery sand,
Ethereal by moonlight, emphasis on the way,
The eye is pleased with this blending sway
Of green hills and copse, wild rocks sweeping the sea,
How long have they waited for someone like me
To acclaim their nature, fall in love with the way
This small bit of Ireland, straddles the green craggy bay.

A SNOW SCENE

Swirling snow, silent flurries whirling around,
Pushing and packing soft flakes on the ground.
Smothering buildings, and any protruding form,
In mounds, and ribbons, to a curved snowy dorm.
Painting a landscape, from black to white,
The drab, the mundane, to a sparkling sight.
A ghostly panorama, with fields of white,
Who dares break the hush, the virginal night?
A white-crowned lamp gives a golden glow,
Making it possible to peer at a shop, with its windows a bow.
If you rub with your hand, along its fast piling ledges,
And lines of falling snow.
The church nearby quickly got its due
Of thick snowy decor from its elegant spire,
Feathered with whirls askew,
To its gargoyles and lintels, and heavy studded door.

Swathing snow, the wind blowing it in trails,
Across the immediate path, and between black spiked rails
Now dotted, and clotted with blobs of white,
Changing the uniform of the night.
For white was the 'in colour' for how long, who would know?
It had come unexpectedly this world of snow.
Roof tops, chimneys, trees near a gate,
All wore white as if waiting a date.
For someone who would deem to walk there alone,
To set the first footprint, for reasons of their own.
Patiently to wait underneath the lamp's gentle glow,
With its illusion of warmth, in this night of cold snow.
Eventually it happened, surging figures did abound,
Breaking the symmetry of the snow glinting ground.

The village of white, earlier silent and bare
Was suddenly alive, people flocked everywhere.
Each doing his or her best not to stumble as they plod
Quickly over the snow, for they weren't sufficiently shod.
Under a sickle moon, frost spiked in the sky,
With a handful of stars winking pertly by.

Lights sprung in windows, but only briefly on show,
Shades were hurriedly drawn, with bed the next step to go.
Each to his own, the pace won't wait,
For sleep claims the weary, whatever the elements dictate.
But when the last shift is over, with the workers all spent,
Nature will work on, to complete her own bent.

Repairing the ravishes that humans leave,
Intricate and sparkling, her own special weave.
A snowy white vista, ethereal, majestic, when captured alone,
Silent beauty to enjoy at dawn.
To fit in and team with a seasonal theme,
A taster of winter, and the first encounter of a Christmas scene.

A SORT OF THANKS

I thank God for giving me this day,
To see in retrospect along life's highway.
Happiness coming from sorrow, with joy,
See the fight to do right, struggle in each girl and boy
When helping and acquiescing becomes a boring ploy.

When inclinations veer the easy way to the end
Of self-preservation, and pleasures that lend
A smug satisfaction in all that you do,
Indifferent to the genuine few.
To have thought for others, if somewhat late,
Shows a hunger, a need to relate.
And need is a beggar, and won't change with the date.

It is no use regretting the past,
The time is now, and tomorrow is a vision of hope, that will last,
Will go on forever, stirring emotions, fighting to free
Love and hatred, seeded in all, and growing in me.
For what and for whom, the secret's locked in the soul,
With treacherous weeds, ready to flower over all.

As the sun shines on a furrow grown old,
Blatant with my footsteps, depressed with cold,
A winter's cold, like the ice around my heart,
When life ended, or so I thought.
When God in His mercy took from me
My partner, my helpmate, leaving me alone and free
To find through my sorrow, new values in life,
Reliving happiness, amidst the heartache and strife.
To be more thankful for then, and now,
To bear with fortitude and help on the way,
Others just like me, thanking God for each day.

A SPECIAL DAY

A languorous feeling made me dawdle awhile,
As from my bed I mused, happy the sun did shine.
No urgencies loomed, this day would be mine,
And later downstairs, I was not surprised at the time.
Switching on the radio, I made breakfast to rhyme,
The music was pleasing, a favourite tune,
And though calm, I felt ecstatic, as high as the moon.

You probe my reason,
Why elated with rapture I enthuse sublime,
Was there a reason, a secret win on the pools?
No but next week it would be welcomed just fine.
But such luck is evasive, a dream never mine.

My well-being still held, irrespective of dreams,
Doing the necessary round, that fits in with my schemes.
For this was the day, to acquiesce not at all,
To one and sundry, aloof I would stay.

Just wishful thinking? Idling would recompense,
Pushing all work out of sight
That cried out for attention,
Which if I saw I might
Forfeit these hours, in my special day,
With its sense of freedom just working away.

I would not delve, or cudgel my brain,
I would do whatever, as I glanced at the window,
Even walk in the rain.
Nothing would deter me, as thoughts flew around,
The first hint of apprehension, quite wearing I found.

Suddenly swamped the enthusiasm in my brain that had allowed
My special day, so strange I felt ecstatic, decidedly cowed
Where was the will to get up and go
That had urged me to do a moment ago?

Had it all been imagination, for a change of scene,
For something, somewhere, that might have been.
That I could still be someone, not me, as I seem,
Just plain black and white, with no variance between.
But part of a rainbow, its colours filling my heart,
A snatch of life, where I would play a part.

I heard myself sigh, was my ego so low?
No, I would not be defeated, I could always sew.
The material was so pretty, it did seem a shame
To let it lie idle, but there was no one to blame.

Just a lonely person craving a special day,
And weaving a dream, making it appear that way.
Playing the usual pretending game,
In a life so ordinary, that everything turns out the same.

A STATE OF MIND

A melancholy silence stretched as far as the eye could see,
It stopped my probe into my tortured soul,
A shifting sequence of sunlight through dancing trees
Adding apprehension, disturbing, frightening,
Why was I here? My befuddled mind was blank,
Wrapped in a cocoon of misery that swamped all thought,
Dulling my senses to place and time.
Without much purpose I stepped onto one of the many stones
Scattered around.
Viewing woods and grassland,
Swivelling a jaundiced eye to massive crags towering on my right,
Eroded and friable with the elements of time.
No inkling of welcome, no touch of warmth, no quarter allowed
For the intruder, who breathed in the chilling moan
Of a sweeping wind.
Hostile was the word that came to mind.
Hostility bristled in every tree, boulder, and blade of grass.
Nature was resigned to her lot,
Indifferent to the burst of intermittent sunshine,
Too weak to stake a claim,
And the pervading silence screamed at me to go.
Forbidding, having no yen for human motion to stir this quiet scene.
My heart missed a beat, palpitating in the uncanny atmosphere.
Swallowing slowly, hardly daring to breathe,
My eyes fastened on swathes of undulating grass,
And remote swaying trees.
Willing myself to shake off this unnatural state,
This dejected fettered stance,
That had me rooted in waves of deep inertia.
Thus immobile, I allowed my sorrow to creep,
Its fluid darts highlighting shocked hallucinations.
Nevertheless the aura was daunting,

Bringing still more conflicting thoughts.
Was the melancholy within my heart distorting this peaceful spot?
With a sigh I walked towards the immediate trees,
Memory telling me a path meandered this evergreen wood,
That would take me home
Rational now, a wash of deeper misery swept over me
As I thought of home.
Would it ever be home again?
Be that as it may I would have to go back
For life held no brief for human sorrow.
The routine of living was heavy, demanding a continuous flow.
Twigs and debris crackled beneath my feet,
I felt numb with cold,
And the hastily donned mac had not much warmth to wrap.
Holly bushes held their glossy sheen,
Having for company fresh green ferns
Splaying softly over mossy mounds.
I was filling my brain now with objective,
Distractions willing my apathy away,
As gazing at clumps of daffodils emerging from their winter's sleep
Splashing golden heads against sombre sheltering trees
Delightful in the sudden burst of April sun.
Pungent earthy smells assailed my nostrils,
Adding to the moment, and the mingling light and shade.
While through a weave of bark and leaves, bluebells grew,
Ready to open each dainty bell.
The fragrance, nostalgic of my childhood days,
Carefree days, exuding happiness with a lyrical dart.
This woodland haze, this soothing hour,
This sweet profusion, with its soft green gaze.
This calm that had swept over me,
This web, that is spinning around my heart,
This tumult of emotions, spraying healing balms to every torn part.
A forever feeling enfolded me with each silent step on leafy ground.
How to explain this moment in time,

With sun-dappled greenery all around.
With sudden piercing shafts lighting a shadowy trail,
Throwing prisms of gold through a verdant veil.
With a rustling song in swaying trees,
Communing with a gentle breeze,
A rhythm was flowing, and I was a part
In a strange dimension, without reason or rhyme,
Somehow I belonged, was suspended in time.
With the damp, sharp smell of woodland around,
Poignant to my senses, I was high off the ground,
Caught in a spiral of green eerie light,
Stretching up to the heavens, to contact someone who might
Take me out of this phenomenon, and rationalise each part
Of over-strung emotions from a broken heart.
Then the moment broke with the sound of a bell,
Or did spirits roam, did they break the spell?
Fantasy stopped with the shrill notes of a bird
Registering as a bell, I thought I heard.
I was now down to earth, to mundane things,
When fluid notes rent the air, the answering call of a mate to share.
The trees grew sparser now, the wind more free,
And across the clearing, an old stone bridge I could see.
It would take me home, back to reality,
As real as the sorrow that had churned my heart,
Which strangely enough now, was resigned to a new start.
The interlude was over, had melted away,
Lost in the fantasy of an unusual day.
Had my feet been guided, well who can say?
But a piece of nostalgia will always creep and flood
When reminiscing at the close of day.
Questions, as if magic, had shown the way,
Mortifying sorrow, for the common good,
With that unforgettable walk, through that evergreen wood.

A THANK YOU IN HOSPITAL
- DIFFERENT STRIDES

Different strides, different walks of life,
Nothing foreseen only of emotions, of pleasure and strife.
Now a new environment, holding back the flow
Of apprehension, of which way to go.
New smells, the atmosphere takes hold,
As trying to assess, to memorise, without being bold.
Stop now, that flow from an overworked brain,
With eyes full of everything, observation's the game.
Nurses in white, with pretty brown legs,
Youth in its glory, for which half the world begs.
Ferns and daffodils pleasure my eye,
With a tiger lily plant, a memory of days gone by,
Calming the hustle and bustle of swift striding feet,
For whatever, or whoever, the deadline to beat.
Different strides that get along fine,
With words of kindness right on time.
The human race in harmony,
The pleasure's been all mine.

Written when in Fairfield Hospital, Bury - Easter 1996.

A TIME THEME

Where does the time go, as to night and day,
As to tomorrow becoming yesterday?
Where is the niche elusively placed,
Ruling our lives, on which dreams are based?
The clock in the hall ticks the hours away,
The quarters, the halves, with midnight having her say,
An unheeded reminder, that this moment in time
Has gone, never more to be mine.
So why all the hatred, culminating in war,
With only so much time to spend here as we are.
When we were young, irrelevant was time,
Life was for living, for lovers in rhyme.
The clock is chiming again, musical and bold,
Why this melancholy with time, is it we know we grow old,
Racing us into a tumult, to destiny's decree,
Pondering time, and what will become of me?
Scanning the heavens, a bird wings by,
So small, so insignificant, in so much sky.
Just as we are, just small specs that be
Part of the Universe, born to be free.
Blindly I cry, seeing its beauty, with a wondrous eye.
Arrogance falling like a worn out cloak,
Humility creeping this spate of time did invoke.
Omissions of the past, a neighbour's needs put on the line,
Compassion a light, a candle to shine.
Would that such things could be, and the chance made mine
To find all my yesterdays, and change all my lost time.

A TOUCH OF SILENCE

A heavenly silence touched all around,
The view softly green, the air sweetly profound.
The breeze was gentle, acknowledging me there,
Warm in its license, ruffling my hair.

I sank onto a boulder to tarry awhile,
Its grey smooth surface veined, in intricate style.
Akin to my mood, laced with thought,
Lacking in substance, needing material sound, I note
This geological structure, part hugging the ground,
Splayed and towering, showing its character around.

Condoning weakness with its beauty, from its niches to spill,
Delicate buds of greenery, waiting to burst and fill
A barren space, a remote rocky face,
With whispers of colour, a softening creation of eye-catching grace.

Lulled into tranquillity I shuttered my brain,
Communing with nature, letting reality drain.
The man-made kind, that wearies the soul,
Where here in silence, it had no goal.

The swathe of grass stirred, holding the moment for me,
An undulating expanse dropping down to the sea,
A soothing surge, its eddying low,
A blend with the silence, its ebb and flow.

The breeze in harmony, swaying a stance of tree,
Rustled in rhythm a song to me.
The musical sequence, lightened the scene,
The blue sky brightening, the sun deciding her face to preen.

Enhancing the silence with her golden smile,
A transient happiness to notch forever in nostalgic beguile.
A piece of God's time given to solitude this day,
To a troubled heart, amidst earthly things, trying to opt away
From life's omissions, such poisonous things,
That rankle, and torment, that turbulence brings.

Finding in nature, in the silent sound,
A soul giving peace on a higher ground.
Where humans can walk with tolerance
And kindness we all can lease,
As man, as nature, create the combined scene,
The will for good must banish, the gathered spleen.

ALL THINGS SPANISH

No books had I read, for time did not allow
The luxury of knowledge to browse and brow.
I did not know what I was missing, for I had never had,
Only slight concepts, rather futile and sad.

Now I envy the sun's rotating pace,
Its daily affinity, to smile on your face.
To traverse your splendours, and the intricate way,
Human elements have lent grace, to your day.

Youth, mine was survival, a fight for life,
To find a niche, in the mundane round of strife.
Beauty was only a stone's throw away,
But common toil sapped the will to seek only the end of each day.

With heart and soul, and breath to the lung,
Acquiesced to the environment, where only the immediate sung.
Thoughts stagnated in the daily round,
With the brain half in limbo, no foreign thoughts could abound.

I found you too late, my sunny Spain,
Now my mind is free to take in your sweet refrain.
I long for your touch, your winter's gentle warm,
Your sensuous nights, and mellow calm.

I cry to the wind sweeping your plains,
Moan your Sierra Nevada's that they, not I,
Saw destiny mould famous, and infamous names.
Miracles of achievement,
Fortitude fraught with deep religious claims.

I resent those years in misnomer spent,
Your evolution, a legend now gratefully lent.
If wishes were horses, beggars would run,
How does it relate, this trite little pun
To my yearnings, and cravings, for this land of Spain,
Where dark handsome lovers, lean and strong men,
Shiver your spine wherever, and when.

I am a beggar, who's found a silver steed,
To fly the air in magic, to appease my need
For a destination Spanish, to dance to a Spanish refrain,
O such happiness you bring me, O sunny land of Spain.

AN EASTER TALE

Mills were silent in Burnley, as in towns all around.
Clattering clogs discarded for a more elegant sound.
It was Easter again, and down Barden Lane
A mix of people hurried, finding common ground
An annual holiday, Pendle Gardens they chose as due
To be of the momentum, to join in the queue
To feed Jack Moor's monkey, with bananas and nuts,
As Sidney Jones, 'Banana King' from his barrow, bananas he cuts
Amidst squeaky favours blown around, as you eat Hot Cross Buns,
Generally baked by most children's mums.
No one o'clock buzzer to call workers back to the mill,
For being Good Friday, and 3 o'clock, everyone's still.
They pause, reverent Lancashire hearts remembering OUR LORD,
And even Jack Moor's monkey held his cage in repose.
The Salvation Army Band played, *'There's a green hill far away'*
Solemn moments, a few tears hastily held at bay.
Afterwards, pop music for roundabouts and swings do the trick,
Someone shouted, "Jack Moor's monkey is going to be sick."
A notice goes up, NO MORE FOOD IN THE CAGE,
And an harassed Jack Moor is exploding with rage.
All part of the Pendle Gardens, and eating more than your fill,
As you sit on the hillside, Jack Moor's monkey is still
The star, the top of the bill.
You laugh it all off, and go with the crowd,
Browsing stalls with trinkets, owners calling out loud.
A witch on a broomstick sailing over the moon,
A brooch, a memento of Pendle Hill and its gore,
Burnley's mentor a secret, at Pendle Gardens and more.

AN EVERETT ODE

It's Kenny Everett, stretching elastic, boggling the mind,
Exploding crackers, bubbling fun his kind
Of nonsensical nonsense, driving you round the bend,
Whoever you are, his is the thing to send,
To captivate, to stimulate
Yearnings evolving, you most recall and enjoy,
Allow with laughter now, though late.
Dreams of childhood gone astray
A foolish ego that fell away.
Dear Kenny, bless him, seems to have the key
To materialise anything for you and me.
His slick jokes quick, his patter loud,
Cut in half, or in a shroud.
A stumping pirate, way back,
To a parrot bowed,
His culture theme becoming topically pat.
The shape can gel, the voice go low,
A writhing ectoplasm, it's Kenny a flow
In space, in lamé, or puffed up in drag,
Kenny whirls, quips, and bounces, no sag, no lag.
A susceptible wardrobe, cobwebs and lace,
Bell, book and candle, a dust-streaked face.
Chains clinking on stones, curtains blown in the wind
A flapping winged bat,
A laughing Cheshire cat.
Dear Kenny, ever right, don't ever rescind.

AN ODE TO IRENE
OF THE RAMBLING OF TIME

Dear Miss Script girl, read this hurl
Of names uncoiling from a dormant furl.
"Yours Irene," is first to roll from the queue,
For Irene was my neighbour, and I give her her due,
A diligent girl, she taught me how to dress-make
In an era much deprived for economy's sake.
Crimping and curling chiffon, gauze curled
With much pinching, and producing a flowery whirl
Of feminine fripperies, when waists were low,
When kiss-curls and the Charleston, and a Cupid's bow
Blended with square-bobbed hair, fringes all a flow.

There was a song about you; it is at the end of the page.
We sang it after the last war in the pubs; it was quite the rage.
Now it's Eileen who has been in the charts,
'Come on Eileen', come on again, you deserve full marks.
Dorothy is nice, and like Eileen is my daughter too,
Being the heroine in my hoped for fame adventures, that grew
Along with the fairies and a green elf, one of the few
Characters in my stories,
I hope you'll enjoy, when I send them to you.
They are somehow in lieu
Of loved ones, now dead and gone,
Loneliness the spur for make-believe, that just goes on and on.
Now Maria is pretty, with Italian charm,
From a land of sunshine, of brown flashing eyes, smiling and warm.
Stella the mother, Markendo the son,
Raven black hair streaking blue as the night,
Lustrous and alive, and catching the light.

Margaret was my cousin, she sang clear as a bird,
But God deemed her an angel,
And heaven the place that her songs should be heard.
Beautiful names like pearls on a string,
The wearer to cherish for the happiness they bring.

Nora, Rosie, Florence and Jane,
Ghosting these moments, and flooding my brain,
From a signature, yours, I imply,
Urging me once more to try
Nostalgia's sweet to while away an hour's schemes,
So is your song my dear, *'Goodnight Irene, Good night Irene'*,
I will see you in my dreams.

AN OLD MINE RAILWAY

An old mine railway, the past in repose
In a forgotten valley bathed in sunset rose.
Shafts of sunlight warmed on an outcrop of stone,
Black remnants of days, glorious and prone
To coal shapes drifting through leafy shade
Now in solitude of yesteryears, by whom they were made.
A Willow sways near a rocky stream,
Heightening moments for secrets, the nostalgic theme.
Silvery catkins burst cotton wool shoots,
Condoning wild briar rose, a spray from roots.
All natural elements, minerals flow,
And coal below.
I follow the path's curve,
My foot steps swiftly on that shady ark, now slow
To the sound of a waterfall
Bringing a bird to drink from its splaying pall
Now ready to sleep under the changing light
Wings a flapping, a silhouette in flight
Negotiating lines of metal
Its silver streak broken,
Where weeds and grasses settle.
An old mine railway, its usage lost with time,
Minus its rhythm, nevertheless sublime.
Guiding a fledgling home to rest
In a world of silence, my breathing the guest,
Giving the past its place to acquiesce its rest,
Its dereliction abhorrent for one of the best.

APPEASING THE HEART

An old world village, mostly timber and stone,
Thatched roofed and shuttered, its humans prone
To dreams and things,
To innuendoes, the daily round brings.
Old folk, young folk, communicating at will,
With children, their dreams, in embryo still.
A place of memory, my emotions rife,
With overwhelming nostalgia, for another life
Urged my feet on the cobbled ground,
My eyes full of everything, the past did abound,
Up the slow rise hill, dry walled like crazy, an elegant snake,
Inviting meander, and what I did make
Of all around, and the recall I had found.
The vantage of light pumped my heart. Silent sound
Was whispering, and said, "Beware!"
As I stood amongst the wild flowers a growing there.
Higgledy-piggledy, thatch and stone, ghostly shapes walking alone.
Futile they cry in the wind's on and off moan.
Houses, shops, a school and the spire
Of the village church, and the old farm byre,
Exuding memories in new dimensions from high on a hill,
Reality a fantasy in the overkill,
A dawn's rosy fingers, expounding my secrets my dreams to fulfil.
Suddenly the sun shines, and gone is the cloud,
The hill is greener, and gone is the shroud
Of nostalgic grey.
I acquiesce to the future, and salute a new day.
I just had to come, and now I must go
From an old world village geared to its own time
Its people awakening happy, feeling sublime

APPRECIATION

A symbol of love, a ring of gold,
Something to cling to when growing old.

Always with you, through the ups and downs of life,
Lady luck per chance, alleviating strife.

Allowing yearnings, with someone sharing your dreams,
A shoulder to lean on, to bolster your schemes.

I pray in the morning, and thank God at night,
For his goodness, and a partner, somehow just right!

For giving us strength to see life through,
Happy together, just me and you.
The same for you friend, I ask sincerely, hopefully too!

AS IT IS

I had a love a long time ago,
But someone deemed that he had to go,
Three children and memories, all exclusive to me,
Have helped life along, with a certain smile I see.
I know he's there, first and last forever to share
The love in our children, in heaven waiting, "God bless him there."
Please Steve play me a love song
For all the happy memories of a once upon a time.
Every night about this time would be appropriate.
There are so many memories I could relate.

A saga so long,
America and Spain caught up in a song
Of happiness, with friends enjoyed on the way.
Time being of the essence, I must stay
My exuberance, and hope and pray
You read my words, for as usual my cat has jumped on my knee
For a stroke and a cuddle.
He is black and called Oscar and is now licking my hand,
In between me adding more info for what I have found
Is a conjuring trick to hold the page high in the air,
As resentfully he just purrs, so beware
Of priorities, especially in cats,
Having tea, or writing a no no.
His performance just catty friendship for me.
But loneliness and memories make for passing time,
And of course a cat,
My lovely Oscar.
I love animals Steve.
We are all God's creatures,
And an animal is for me so sublime!

BLACK MONDAY

I had been in bed for hours tossing and turning. Midnight had come and gone, and the small hours ticked audibly by. As a last resort I turned wearily onto my stomach, which often proved the most comfortable position to be, after plumping up my pillows a bit. Thus stretched out I waited for blessed sleep.

Suddenly the room was deathly cold, and the air was pregnant with an electric sound. Petrified I held my breath, and in this mystic aura I felt hands grip me on both sides of my hips. My heart was in my mouth, my urge was to scream, but no sound came, for my voice seemed to have left me.

The unknown hands slipped up over my back, then gripped down on my hips again and icy fingers repeated the process yet again. I was now sweating with fright, my mouth felt so dry that I could not have cried out for my life, as hysterical thoughts now filled my brain.

"Had a loved one had a terrible accident?" Many thoughts mingled with other terrible thoughts, but as suddenly as they had come, the fingers and hands were gone. I moved and breathed a sigh in blessed relief, then fell into a few hours of sleep.

Next day an unexpected caller arrived at my house. Well two people in fact. I heard my daughter call as she walked up the lobby. She had my sister-in-law Helen in tow.

I was so pleased to see them both as visitors on a Monday were somewhat rare. I beckoned them both to be seated, but my daughter just stood near the sofa, with a solemn-looking face. Her quiet look, and something in Helen's face triggered off alarm bells in my mind. Seated now I waited as Helen seemed about to speak.

I spoke first, "Is it Stephen?" He was my brother and her husband.

With a slight shake of her head she said, "I got your Dorothy to come along to break the sad news to you. Doris died early this morning. She was rushed into hospital only yesterday but she deteriorated so quickly. We were called being her nearest contact."

"It was black Monday," I thought. I just looked into the fire, going over my experience of the earlier hours. When I pulled myself together a little I just said, "Yes I know, she was with me last night."

Our Dorothy, never one for much conversation shouted, "Mother!" with bewilderment on her face.

I told them both later of the hands laid upon me, and the shock and fright I had felt, and would remember forever. "It was our Doris, my sister, who had come to me when she passed away."

She had left behind her a husband who was blind due to a brain haemorrhage, that was why my sister-in-law Helen, had come to tell me. I asked God to rest my sister's soul, and prayed for her husband Leonard, who would now need help all around. It was indeed black Monday.

My little sister Doris, who I had helped to bring up, and loved and cared for as deeply as if she was my own child, had come to say goodbye.

As I said before I will never forget that moment. You read of such things and brush them away, thinking that they can't be true. But when it happens to you, then you surely know that someone is really there with you, and your guardian angel will always show you the way.

BRIEFLY NEW YORK

I was whisked down a boulevard. I had dreamed of being in a car, full of impatience, honking to go. The driver's baleful eye daring me to voice my apprehension, a stifled cry at his swift manoeuvre, hurtling us by.

The hustle was mundane, the street vendors, their abode slightly peculiar, but I allowed the code of buying and selling, each to his own. Having waited a lifetime, who was I to moan?

The yellow taxi honked again, timed with a jump from a too eager starter producing a bump. It was at the street sign, *'Park Avenue'*, which was quite an elegant start to my brief tour going around New York.

In my mind a picture visualised from the screen. If only my eyes could x-ray the concrete and steel, that scintillating glass of decor, the elite of the jet set, allowed their dreams. I would glean, but I was on the outside making the best of my schemes.

Broadway had me despondent, I had built up and lost, for my imagination was too vivid, but perspective steadied the cost. I longed to tarry, to pause for a while, till the night sky grew purple, and the stars strove to shine, on this neon splendour the lights of man-made array, this kaleidoscope of grandeur turning night back to day.

I was too late for Tiffany's barely reached the first floor, when staff packed me politely down to the last open door. Degrees of satisfaction had me carry on, so hooked was the taxi driver, his inhibitions long since gone.

Acquiescing my questioning, and urging me on to Forty-second Street, Fifth Avenue with flags a flare, to Rockafella's Plaza and fountains, and weirdoes with hair.

One more cruise, pinnacles high, the Empire State Building I glimpsed on the right passing by. Repressed emotions palpitating my heart, the aura of East Side, West Side, and State, mingled with overhead transport, and had manifest the bait.

For exhilaration, for curiosity, and my heart's sake, I will briefly do the take of New York, New York.

Briefly assessed New York yes, named twice, New York.

CHANGING TIMES

This is a tale of Lancashire life,
Along with the heartache, the struggle and strife.
Burnley, yes around Whittlefield, I was born and bred,
But will anyone recollect when I'm gone and dead?
On the lives of the people, their customs, their style,
Their motivation with interest, to refer it on file.

Maybe no one will care about life spent that way,
And what I could tell you, would take nearly all day.
We were "Poor as Lazarus," I used to hear Mam say,
But clean with it, and on occasions gay,
With restricted views in our part of the world,
No wireless, no telly, for far-flung fields to be unfurled.

The most that folks got up to in the way of a treat,
Was to pay a penny for a Mid-day, used by half of the street
To pick out a winner, a horse with hope to aspire,
To win money for a drink, a nosh, or a different attire.

Of course there was sex, but in a more subtle way,
And what folks got up to, well I'd rather not say.
They went boozin', came home sloshed, and threw t' furniture about,
And after a big fight with the wife, got many a clout,
Black Maria would come to sort it all out.

Those good old days are now bulldozed away,
Like the stones, bricks and mortar, flattened and levelled to make way
For a new way of life, via a new motorway.
It runs on and down, and right through our street,
Irrespective of nostalgia, from the old and the few,
It's demolished corners where people did meet,
Quietening forever the voice no one could beat.

It's been planned and calculated to the last curve and sweep,
With black tarmacadam, shiny and new,
So pardon me for reminiscing, it just tends to creep,
And there's a bus if I hurry, to take a last peek
At the land around the Whittlefield of the day,
Before these modern constructors sweep my memories away.

CLOGS AN' T' MILL

Clogs were t' most worn footwear of t' day
When I was a kid, an' if yer lived down our way,
Sunday night it was a ritual, yer set too wi' a will
Cleanin' all t' clogs for t' school, an' fer t' mill.
Brushin' and rubbin', wi' blackin' an' spit,
Finishin' shine off wi' t' velvet, allus there in t' kit.

I can see miself now, sat on t' fender doing me stint,
Wi' a clog in mi' hand, givin' me mother a broad hint,
Fer I longed ta dash out, ta follow t' crowd,
To join in an' sing wi' t' Salvation Army band loud.
You cud jump an' mek sparks when yer clog irons were new,
Aye, an' slur wi' a run, when nearly worn out too.

Slidin' down hill, then runnin' back,
By gum it was fun, on that slippery track.
But not fer our Mam, when we'd slurred 'em all out,
Fer there was so little money, we had hardly owt
Fer a new set meant money at Cloggers ta find,
An' that was a near miracle, in them days o' kind.

Fer we had ta join t' Co-op Club ta get owt new,
Payin' a shillin' a week, fer each pound due.
Yes 'Mutuality Club' did help, as a lot o' folks found,
But yer waited three weeks, fer t' cheque ta cum round.
Leavin' school at fourteen, I joined workers at mill,
Me clogs soundin' hollow across yard,
Wi t' skips an' t' warehouse, musty an' still,
Wi' t' bales o' cloth, wi' some on t' table waitin' ta be picked,
Fer loose ends an' floats, scratched up an' then ticked
Wi' t' details in a ledger, cluttered onta sill,
Wi' bobbins an' an oil can, an' a brew tin measuring a gill.

An' hangin' by its flap woz an old cloth cap,
An' yer knew whoever owned it, wud surely be back.
Yer went early at dinnertime, back ta t' mill, ta do what woz due,
But mostly ta savour, an' get yer fill o' latest gossip, always on cue!
Past th'engine hole, where steam power was all fed,
On through all t' factory, turnin' wheels on their bed
Of well oiled straps, leathers strong an' wide,
An' woe betide the body who too near them did glide.

Pushin' t' door open on that hot cotton smell,
Steam is heard hissin' from pipes wi' holes in as well,
Ta keep th'air humid, sprinklers spray all
Th' immediate around from wall ta wall.
Fer when th'engine gets goin', stiflin' it wud be,
But bikinis weren't thought of, only now by me.

Wheels in motion now whizzed, beltin' noise low ta high
Wi' t' pickin' sticks hittin' shuttles across t' weft an' back by,
Weavin' cloth wi' a vengeance, each Lancashire loom,
Wi' t' workers stretchin' an' reachin', in that small bit o' room
Allotted ta each thread, ta flow twice through each reed,
From under t' right rod, ta just t' right yell.
First an' third, second an' fourth, woz what a weaver knew well,
Woz t' sequence ta tek ends up, yer strived fer like hell,
Wi' just right essential care an' speed,
Fer a perfect piece o' cloth ta pass a jaundiced eye,
Of yon crotchety clothlooker, an' don't ask me why?

Sweating an' toilin', all busy onta t' ground,
To a stranger all hell cud not be more profound.
Fer t' noise woz terrific, an' t' temperature too,
In that frenzy o' work, wi' no time fer a brew.
An' if thy were covin', and a tenter thy'd be,
Tha woz harassed by thi boss, ever watching thee.

Fer tha had ta put th'edin afooar an' after t' mark,
Get piece off quickly, an' lap a new start.
Yer got used ta t' noise, learned ta talk in mime, readin' folk's lips
An' yer got along fine, till yer boss caught yer at it,
Then a kick below t' shin
Made yer thank God fer yer clogs, that were as thick as t' din.
Yer had bin talkin' through, when yer woz caught,
So on wi' yer weavin', his bite belied his bark,

Now time fer sweepin', woz when t' weft run smooth,
Or on a tea break, when only people did move.
When t' looms were silent, an' covered in snow,
They just had ta be brushed, row after row.
No paid sweepers in them days, yer did yer own yer see,
An' sometimes from yer boss yer got a small fee,
Or from those not so agile, or not so keen
Ta get oiled up, an' fluffed up, where t' down had been.

Fer it flew in yer hair,
Got piled everywhere,
Smothering' yer clogs, thickening yer apron string,
So yer could hardly find where yer scissors an' reedhook did swing.

Then weavin' along wi' yer hand onta slay,
Yer prayed th'ends stayed up, fer it woz late inta day.
But th'air woz so dry, yer cud hardly breathe,
An t' sprinklers had stopped, an' now tempers wud seethe.
An' many a prone body o'er aloom yer did see,
Tryin' ta beat clock, bein' nearly home time, an' fer tea.
Wheels then slowed ta a grindin' halt,
The silence so loud, it always gave you a jolt.
Well that woz that, another day done,
Yer turned yer loom over, or left it, as some.

As shudderin' in yer sweat, glad ta be on yer way,
Fer yer'd worked from dawn ta end o' day,
Yer gathered up yer coat, picked yer bag up from t' floor,
Then walked up t' broad alley, a makin' fer t' door.
Yer clogs clatterin' through t' warehouse, wi' their usual air,
Wi' th' occasional loiterer, just fiddlin' there,
Adjustin' his cap, or maybe fillin' his pipe,
Before swiftly leggin' it, through t' door out o' sight,

Home over t' cobbles, clogs cloppin' away,
As did tongues o' some workers, mekin' up fer all t' day
A bit o' scandal had irked them, burstin' ta voice their say,
Aye, who wud be a weaver? I say, just let t' chance cum,
Aye, who wud wear clogs?
Well maybe not many, but there'd always be some!

COME HOME

There comes in the wind, a voice in the wind
Bating my breath on the long way home,
Crying a river, a million tears,
With the years of longing in its singing moan.
"Come home my love, I want your return,"
The stars and moon's impatient, the heavens sigh.
The night's alive with your voice.
In the wind as it passes by.
Your name's in repeat, the theme the same,

A heart's yearning acquiesce, to taking the blame.
Love is all, embraces all, all of you
In all I do.
Turbulent emotions with the voice I hear,
The voice in the wind, me calling you home,
Wanting you, calling out, calling you near.
"Come home my love, I need you manifest for which I was born,
A soul's persistent peregrination, defeated and torn.
Bursting emotions, deep as the ocean's perpetual surge,
Come home my love, come home for all time,
Equated our love to merge sublime."

COMPASSION
(Written when the Falklands War broke so many hearts)

Invaded soil, a windswept plain, a sorrowful task,
But who shall we blame?
For the nameless crosses, of only God knows who,
Slain for what? The arrogant few.
In patriotic duty, killing the order, with no questions why?
Glorious youth's destiny, there's no shame if you cry.

For life at its best, swept away on war's crest,
Leaving broken hearts, wondering where a loved one fell,
Where a loved one rests?
A travesty of greed, under an alien sky,
With no succour for those doomed to die.
God bless those lads, British and Argentinian all,
And God bless those doing the caring, where they did fall!

CONSOLATION

Feelings are sensuous with nothing to hold,
Nothing tangible, only a shape of gold
You gave me, and thoughts of life,
Put into words that cut like a knife.
Reminisce holds everything your world did behold,
A million secrets locked in your soul.
In this inadequate state, hiding in emptiness revealing all
To the lonely figure, waiting chance to live again,
To rekindle emotions, surely insane!
Placing tangible memories in a timeless light
Of rising happiness, a will-o-the wisp of right.
Once you belonged, was half of a pair
Of loving arms, but you're no longer there.

COMTEMPLATION

Gnats dance at twilight; the sun dips
In a haze of rosy cloud,
Thoughts dally in reverie, stab at dreams floating high
In a thistledown shroud.
Another day on the wane
Quietly passing away,
The smell of the forest mingling
With the smell of new bunched hay.
Verdant spires in the sky
Sway in unison ready to sleep,
A tranquil vale dripping shadows,
Where lovers can meet.
Nocturnal life a surging,
Acclaiming their time,
The beating heart of man quickening
To nature's rhythm and rhyme.
A stately home, its stance in measured repose,
On soft sprung turf, curbed with gravel, and wild briar rose.
Inviting to the wanderer, its ancient door and mellowed stones,
Mysteries of the past pervading, as the silence moans.
Fingers of grey now congealing to a darker hue,
The settling sun and the twilight, having had their due.
An owl breaks the silence to-wit to-woo,
The wind whistling through the woodland, answers right on cue!
Rustling trees a whisper, a rabbit scurries away,
The stately home commanding, preening its face,
Its windows opaque, scintillating with grace,
Blending with nature, and man's thoughtful pace.
In the moon's swift gilding, of this quiet spot,
Conjuring romantic secrets in happy bivouac
In phantom shadows of silver light
Acquiescing the beauties of the night.

DECISIONS

'Sapient smells wafting on the breeze
Of rain-drenched fauna and dripping trees
Pungent on the cool night air,
Permeating breath with nature's flair.
Soft mellow thoughts, piercing the heart,
Senses brimming, humanity caught
In the main stream of life,
Friction eternal, the moment rife.

A sliver of moon deigned to glide this deep purple orb
Of slumbering heavens, fraught with probe.
A golden glow streamed from a house of stone,
A symbolic beacon for hope to atone.
A wisp of smoke coiled in the silent air,
Home was imminent, and she was there.

DOWN OUR STREET

Down our street, so many times you say,
When speaking of days so far away,
Lightening the moment, to go over your lot,
With all the nothingness around, for that's all you had got.
The character with the smile on his face, walking with his current gait
The air blue, flashing his deserts and dues from a long past wait.
Lothario's game, love 'em and leave 'em.
Sparked gossip that was no surprise with the games and bets on
"Annie, up for anything in her own backyard."
Young and swaggering she had his card.
New faces gave work for idle tongues to flick
In quick rapport, or in disdain to spit.
For one Lothario it turned out well,
Who had who on a string, who did the sell?
Well they got together, but of the bit in-between
There is gossip enough of what folks have seen.
Nothing new down our street,
Innuendo maybe, of what has been.

DRIFTING THOUGHTS

Small facets of life dance along the breeze,
Slivers of silver, and shafts of gold,
Catching the sunlight, piercing my soul.
Memories drip from corners of recall.
A baby's cry, a velvety rumpled face,
Tiny fists dithering, waiting a mother's embrace
With towelling and talc, as ablutions take place.
Sweet, the nostalgic roll
Of music, takes over the strings as they fall
On a certain time, that long ago place,
Before your eyes, the smile and the face
No surprise, happiness is without beguile,
Strife accepted, the moment's style.
Lives, Dunkirk a sacrifice, free, awaiting joy,
A God-given ploy,
With the wind of change, the destiny all can see
The immediate resigned to being what you are,
The common threads of ordinary me.

EVEN A KING

The time was conductive to a magic spell,
Settled in reverie, a lamp, a genie, and a wishing well.
His Imperial Majesty, wrapped in mythology and dreams,
Trod infinite halls and balconies of awe.
Secrets rising from far away time,
Human relevance, an elixir of enchantment of fascinating schemes.

Dragons ensconced in haunts of gold, fuming fire,
Flaming flames embroiled with power and lusting desire.
Ethereal cities gleaned in rotations wed in
Whirls red, magenta bursting, midnight blue,
Unsuspecting fingers clawing through
Nebulous shapes, concubines robed in lures of silk,
Celestial chemistry in clouds of milk.

The Bridge of Sighs, The Empire State,
Serpents in mosaic, sea pink wenches wait
To obviate, in a more tangible state.
The Royal debacle tiring, phenomena drifts away,
The night's potential allows a bright new day.

A crown sits on a cushion, jewels on purple,
Tasselled and ready to sleep,
Immune to the fantasies dreamers strive to keep.
Vines, flowers and riot, figures dance still
Playing destiny's game, giving emotions their fill.

A drum beats in slow rhythm, words scrolled in red ink,
A shimmer of water inviting the brain to drink.
On wells of iniquity I climb the golden stair,
Turmoil, tranquillity, Father Time in obeisance waits a mortal there.

His Imperial Majesty sleeps,
The witching hour in limbo.
A new dawn, in motion all secrets, keeps.
Sweet the sunrise, sweet the memories to date,
Sweet the maid proffering coffee, sticky and hot.
Sweet His Imperial Majesty's smile, conjecture sweet,
Yes so sweet, for all she had got.

FAR AWAY TIME

Where are the meadows I played as a child,
Such carefree happy days, under skies blue and mild,
Where swathing grasses, with Clover growing at will,
Swayed in the wind a silent motion, sweeping to the rise of a hill,
Exuding an aura, a whispered lure growing loud,
Inviting trespass into that flower-filled shroud.

Field after field of Buttercups in the sun,
The gradient later enforcing a quickening run,
To where a stream flanked with Mayflowers thread its way
Through banks of bracken and trees, bursting in May.
A splayed riot of blossom, with Violets hidden away.
Shy and demure leaves hugging the ground,
Dainty and dewy, all purple gowned.

Happy roaming, exploring days, bare brown feet on a sandy track,
Crossing stiles and meadows, with the sun on your back.
Now dug up and churned up, transport ruling the day,
Demanding ribbons of road, a tarmacadam way.
With roundabouts, and signs standing rigid and new,
Giving directions where once blossom trees grew.

Directing a child's fancy, in its own little world
Of nature, where fantasy's unfurled.
Where a shower of rain came from a witch's brew,
And had you sheltering in the woodlands, where tall bluebells grew.

But when the sun shone again,
And with the resilience of youth,
It started all over the make-believe game,
With your friends you are a Princess, with spells revealed in rhyme,
Exciting hours of pretend, in fairyland time.

Improvising till tired, till the sun has gone,
When hastily you gather, now tired now the sun has gone,
You collect a wild flower bouquet to carry home anon,
To stick in glass jars in the yard,
Where it is not very hard
To make a back street into a meadow, rounding off your day,
Making a home on a terrace, a lighter shade of drab grey.

FOREVER MEMORIES OF MY BURNLEY

So many memories of a far away time, the good and bad relived, in nostalgic rhyme. People and places, some lost in the role of life's commitments, death, and the years taking their toll.

A certain street, a lamp's gleam in the dark, a lane where lover's walked, eyes full of soul, full of heart. A figure, a face comes through the vale of time, the immediate is the past, the aura is tangible, the happiness sublime. You walk again on cobbled streets, with nowhere particular to go, the wind is in your hair, your clogs now hurting you so. For work was zero in that era of life, each street with its sorrows, trying to hide with reticence the trouble and strife. Indulging in dreams, anticipation the key to golden days, just happy to be me.

From Whittlefield to Burnley Lane I tramped many a day, down West Gate, with Massey's Brewery filling the air with the stench of beer brewing all of the way. Direct, no indirect, knocking on the doors of the elite, nearly begging for cleaning work, to lift my heart, and more than not my oh so aching feet! Hunger the spur, where pride takes a back seat. For oh to be free from that terrible means test, where weekly with others you stood in a backyard in Stoneyholme, waiting to go through the door to collect your voucher for the bare necessities of life, and nothing more.

And as ever it went on, the daily round. You saw the Co-op horses in splendid array, tasselled and feathered for the First of May. Processions scraped from nowhere, to fill your heart. From Padiham through Burnley, the Brass Bands a part, with music and banners and children in white. With the rain miraculously held back, making everything right. Girl Guides and Boy Scouts, the old guard and the new, having hoped and prayed with the pious few.

Rows of houses and mills were solid on the ground, a sprawling pattern of terraces and walls of stone, drab and uniform, all in sombre tone. From the Mitre to Gannow Top and Accrington Road, with easy access to Coal Clough Lane and Manchester Road. The thread so versatile, you had to be in the know, of bridges and ginnel, steps shortening the way to the Irish Park, Top o' Town, St. Peter's Church and the Cannons, sharing common ground. A grim reminder of the First World War, and sadly reclaimed in the Second, with iron railings to swell again the Arsenals of War.

Whilst the Leeds and Liverpool Canal wound its impressive way bringing horse-drawn barges to rest on the Cut bank floor. A regular stop was Bank Hall Pit, with many more galore at mills weaving cotton, whose engine holes and chimneys were the beginning and the end of steam power. Keeping the wheels turning, keeping King Coal burning, keeping hope afloat in Lancashire hearts.

They were well known for coping with adversity in the 20's and 30's, their destiny a jigsaw of strife, of love, laced with the quick rapport from the endless pool of Lancashire wit, always ever ready when searching for the elusive part, the moment to fit. When soup kitchens with broth and bread doled out were a Godsend in time, ambrosia from heaven and savoured like wine, as crossing the road from Barlow's Chemist succulent aromas rose, churning heart and stomach to be on time.

From the Mitre, along Trafalgar to Manchester Road, for town was a long track, making one think of another way to go around. To walk the stone steps to the meadows you turned half way back, cutting over glass-roofed mills and the canal, sluggish and slack, tired of effluence from Sandygate, where Watt's clock tower, a timeless eye, was a watcher of mill workers' toing and froing by.

Clattering clogs were unisex, differentials showing on Sundays. A young maid with shoes flaunts her wraps at the chaps. Lads in skittish mood abandoning their old flat caps. Innuendoes would fly about later when on the 'Drag' they would go. All the eligible folk of Burnley paraded through the centre of town. Gangs favoured their own side, full of exuberance up to Colne Road their beat could be found. Boys and girls giving and catching the eye of love's young dream as the weekend went by. And as Correlos shop was the cheapest for a ready-made suit, many a dandy in a trilby filled the bill, a real beat!

At the Palace and 'Vic' we had a pantomime, the first talkies at the Empire were fascinating and fine. On the corner of Cow Lane,

Tognerallas had the best ice-cream in town, with 'Pea Bob's' next door if your coppers stretched around. But no dawn did brighten the way to the mill, or the 'knocker-up's' rattle on bedroom windows, bringing reality for the mind to drink its fill.

There was no warmth either in that warehouse piled high with cloth that was musty and still. Waiting our fate we hung around in small groups, there was no need for queues, hoping to catch the eye of the Manager, and prepared to lick his shoes, just to be picked, if only to work for a day, to help scrape through the poverty, to help pay your way. But the elements were missing to lift a body's will, and in those worrying moments, time stood still, inevitable and solid like a wall of doom. Would you find favour and walk into that busy workroom? And if you were lucky, would you be back after dinner as the one o'clock buzzer did boom the regular time signal heard in the air, bringing hurrying clogs back to the mill, with precision and flair.

But seasons still changed, immune to all strife, and love still blossomed in Burnley, giving birth to new life. Easter holidays were the first break, always sunny and bright, and trekking down Barden Lane to Pendle Bottoms was a cure all right. All the town seemed suddenly light-hearted, as the Easter ritual got on its way, with everyone enjoying the shops, roundabouts, catch-pennies and swings.

Jack Moore's monkey was the main attraction, and was fed on bananas and nuts that the children did bring. You danced if you wanted, music filling the air, you felt content on the hillside in a place selected with care, as water trickled in ridges a dry spot was indigenous to sit and eat your hot cross buns, most likely home-made by hard-working mums.

The Salvation Army Band did the honours at three o'clock after the pause. They boomed out with, '*There is a Green Hill Far Away*'. A few minutes of remembrance that no one did flout. Acknowledging the occasion the big wheel's sphere just flew. Laughter and screams descending, enjoyment given its due. Grown-ups and children queued up for the fun, parents the foremost, trying not to be outdone.

Now Towneley Hall, Burnley's heritage of Elizabethan charm, was a spot to be revered. Its plants and woodlands so sylvan, its grandeur so calm. Most Sundays, with friends I walked to Towneley through town, where ghosts and secrets we knew did abound. Listening in awe of the message left on the skeleton, hundreds of years in the gloom, that disintegrated when a caretaker fell into the room.

The room was really a dungeon, part of a priest's hole, the whole being a tunnel to St. Mary's, the secret hidden in the church wall. There were figures and paintings gracing the corridors of stone, and cases of birds, medals and pottery were everywhere, and towering in a corner, stood a great brown bear. I learned of India and Honduras, where our forefathers did roam. Seeing the trophies around me that they had brought home.

But it was the chapel that was special, oak panelled and bare, with no flower on its altar, petered black with age, its solitude spreading the aura of no one to care. Its statues knowing the secrets the past had whispered there. Passed a settle now and a tallboy, the same oak age, as richly carved as the baby's cradle, and more like a cage, stood Queen Anne's bed, on a carpet still fresh and in one piece, so delightfully Persian, my wonder never did cease.

In its own showcase at the top of the stairs, the Taj Mahal was housed. It was an Eastern ivory so rare, where people stopped and browsed and wondered why a Japanese lady should sit with a fan to her face, so demure and so shy. I let out a sigh as we took a last look at the woodlands, and being spring, just over the brook, bluebells, so heavenly pungent and sweet vied with daffodils, yellow frilled, trying hard to compete.

Pendle Hill with its witches, Hambledeon Hill and Roughlee, you had a choice for your fun if you decided to come. With Hollingworth Lake at Easter, a much taken run. But Shanks's Pony was mediocre for me, truly the only way to anywhere, irrespective of the pun.

Our annual holiday was always the first week in July, the end of which the Cattle Market supported the Burnley Fair. And I have seen it hailstone when hurrying down there from the Mitre, down Westgate, across the centre of town to keep a date with roundabouts, big boats and a coconut shy, with the Fat Lady and boxing booths catching the eye. Walking over steam pipes trailing the ground, the smell of oil and candyfloss significantly profound. The Wurlitzer Organ's glamour and music lifting your feet, cold and sleet no deterrent for this special treat. And the ghost train I have ridden on with a current young man, full of elation and romance, emotions taking you to heaven, cancelling all fright, for with those strong arms around you, everything seemed all right.

Memories that drip, that swamp your brain, triggered off by an old song's haunting refrain. Small idiosyncrasies, a certain time, a place, let nostalgia creep, illuminates a face.

Happy the moment, reminiscence filling the hour in beautiful reverie, retrospect making it flower. Sorrow and strife in surprising low key, for the sting has all gone, leaving only me wallowing in the years of the changeless past, a rosy ball of memories. My forever Burnley, as long as I shall last.

GETTING IT RIGHT

Just forget for a while your mop and broom,
Using spit and polish in and out of each room.
Just sit and relax, learn how to smile,
Let your anxious brow, smooth out for a while.

Feel tenseness flow like summer rain,
As changing your mood, you dust out your brain.
Just sweep the cobwebs from niche and nook,
With resulting clarity, like a knowledgeable book.

A book of dreams, to which you once did thrill,
That filled your heart, and moulded your will.
You were the kingpin, made your own time,
Dancing through moments, warm and mellow as wine.

Remember it all, what you planned to do,
Away from the mundane, just one of the few
Gossamer webs, weaving a coil,
Capturing life's dreams, definitely a foil.

What quenched the torch, where did the dreams go?
What were you to be, one of the elite, with riches a-flow?
When did love blossom, with the prior claim,
Making a shambles of the path marked 'FAME'.

Love me forever, so worthwhile all is well,
But have the threads tautened, the time is now to tell.
As reminiscence flows, nostalgia having its will,
Let this restful hour bring happiness,
Pruning your heart of dreams that you tried to kill.

GOING BACK

The same Savannah, isolated from the marauding world,
Stretching neath a sky unfurled
Like a painted canvas, with the clarity of light
Mixing colours that blend with the shadows of night.
Watered by tears way down the age,
A Nomad's land, where the Gods spewed up their rage.
Harbouring visions of dead and gone love,
Imbued immortal in the time book above,
With a wafted aura, from each well-worn page.
Grasses and flowers ready to sleep in the breeze,
Cornflowers, blue, the sweetest I'd seen.
Buttercups and clover blushing red,
Sprang from the good earth and soft grassy bed.
Trees towered high,
A back cloth in the sky,
Adjusting with dignity the hill's gentle roll,
Whilst spreading their cloak near an old stone wall.
A verdant profusion, with a rustling song
Whispering an answer to the cheep cheep along
Lengthening shadows enhanced light and shade,
And a silvery stream, knowing how to behave,
Turned its rippling waters a deeper hue,
To complement the sky's changing blue,
Blending pink with mauvey grey,
Shooting fingers of indigo to end the day.
I picked my way over the sparse-trod track,
Whilst a tumult of emotions carried me back.
Pushing on further, neath a low hung bough,
My feet lent a purpose, walking quicker now,
Negotiating the hollow round the curve of the hill,
With my eyes in remembrance, drinking their fill.

I was fighting nostalgia, for the past came back strong,
A cloak of memories unfolding and lingering along.
For love I had found and buried near
This old stone Kirk that had beckoned me here.
The waning sun filtered the trees,
Blazening a window with its dying light.
The same sun, the same window, but on a far away night.
It put to shame the weathered door,
Inviting me in to kneel and pray on the cold stone floor,
Streaked with the flow of rain down the years,
Somehow akin to my unshed tears.
The door creaked inward, pervading a musty smell,
It smote my nostrils, sharp like a bell,
As forward I walked over dank dark stones,
Passing pews and panelling blackened with age,
Into a shaft of sunlight that gave warmth to my bones.
I gazed at the altar, and candelabra still there,
Where my bride had knelt with me, her life to share.
As I have said, the same sunlight had proclaimed the end of that day
Through the same window, in just the same way.
The two young lovers, vowing never to part,
Wrapped up in dreams, with love in their hearts.
But Nemesis stalked, riding hard on our heels,
We had prayed for escape, allowing the way we did feel.
The fury of war thundered over the hill,
The bomb, swift and relentless, I hear it still.
A vacuum sucked my emotions away,
And I cried out in anguish, "Why did *she* have to pay?"
I knelt on the spot where she had stood,
I wanted to pray, if only I could,
To that Mystic Presence, that had called me back,
To lay the tumult, which in my being did rack
Every minute of every waking day,
Torturing my soul, taking my heart away.

Suddenly an aura was there all around,
In this old Kirk, where brief happiness I'd found.
The walls, the altar, were casting a spell,
And someone was with me, I know, I could tell.
I prayed then for peace in my heart to quell
The sorrow and yearnings, that made living a hell.
I gave thanks for the moment, for me being part,
Of this mystical awareness, that had touched my heart.
Words cannot describe how I felt kneeling there
In the twilight shadows, bereft of all care.
I heard a whisper, and a candle shone bright,
Or would you say it was the wind, and the sun's dying light,
Sweeping the last of its rays out of sight,
Before sinking its face in the folds of the night.
I rose in the gloom, made for the creaking door,
Tranquillity had come as I knelt on the floor.
Across the Savannah, she had called me back
To this old stone Kirk, off the beaten track,
And the swaying trees darkened the night,
But I was born anew, all around me was light!

GRATEFUL SPECULATIONS

A winter's day, biting wind spiked with frost and snow,
The room is cold, and your bones tell you so.
As huddled in layers of acrylic wear,
Shivering you strive to stretch and pull
A cardigan around you,
And think of the days when garments were either cotton or wool.
No newfangled man-made stuff,
Just sheepy curls, the genuine stuff,
That were as warm as toast, making you sweat and puff.
That you could spin and eventually lash into pots of dye,
The concoction your own,
Which did surely vie
With other garments, home-made to tone.

So poking up the fire, you hope for the best,
While straining your cardigan around your chest.
Then the chiming clock, a diversion in time,
Brought a friendly face near, heart-warming and fine.
The lonely hours were behind you, had faded away,
And feeling relaxed you stretched out and lay
In the height of comfort, settee close to the fire,
With the telly to view, till to bed you retire.

A touch of magic had entered your room,
With today's technology banishing yesterday's gloom.
After a while hunger makes you stir,
And in a shivering huddle you walk away
Into a cold kitchen to brew some tay.

Quickly it is done,
Then with a snack back you come,
To enjoy it with what is left of your day.
To resume your viewing with a settled calm,
The brew giving warmth, the snack a satisfying balm.
Along with your layers of acrylic wear,
When a sudden newsflash is being spoken there.
Horrific tragedy, making you stare
Gratefully round your well-worn room,
Trying to visualise it being a rubble-strewn tomb.
Shuddering with the thought, it could have happened to you,
Momentarily distracted, the news still new.

Speculative thoughts tumble in your brain,
The accident bringing past sorrows back plain.
If only this, if only that, you muse on things no longer there,
Substitutes, as in life, making do,
As with garments that were once wool too.

Shivering you sigh, wrapping yourself more tightly
In your far from adequate acrylic wear,
The fire needs mending, but you continue to view.
Compared with tragedy, cold is nothing to bear,
You really are one of the fortunate few!

HAPPY HOURS HAPPINESS TO ME

Little sheep faces looking at me,
So pretty in their expectations of where to be.
The gate is open, will they go through,
As Meg in the grass, gives them her due
For a definite lift, as she hustles, and how,
Following her shepherd's lead and whistle, to which to bow.
All nature compact with the wind everywhere,
Whispering, rustling, one man and his dog, beware, beware!

Happy reflections, all emotions chill,
With little sheep faces still looking at me,
And a black and white Collie, in the picture still.
With voices of satisfaction following me over the hill.
A place of nature and animals, my heart happy and trill,
One man and his dog with the moment, the accent, the will.

HAPPY THOUGHTS

Ribbons of thought weaving away,
Ambitions, romance, colourful and gay.
Languor of time, fluid and free,
Swathing the brain, resting the eye, painting vistas that be,
Clear and beautiful, as on the arc of a rainbow,
You climb thistledown light.
In euphoric moments, a sensuous delight.

Secrets flowing from your innermost soul,
Pounding your heart, as you see your goal.
Suspended moments, making a part of your day
Something special, with happiness holding sway.
Each to his own, you probe a celestial plain,
A pleasurable high, a place of gain.
If only dreams were reality, manifesting to stay,
Ribbons of happiness, weaving a beautiful day.

HEARTBREAK

I have a letter I treasure more than gold,
It's rather dog-eared and tatty, for it's now very old.
When I first read it, I thought how sincere and true,
But time proved otherwise, as the details would, if you knew.
It had been in my bag more than half of my life,
Lying with documents and papers, secrets, happiness and strife.

This particular letter of so long ago,
Could relate as much now, for things are still as much so.
It's an apology for negligence, not of word but of deed,
Of when sick and needing people, I got this letter to read.
The writer saying how sorry, how selfish she had been,
That soon I would see her,
I knew up and down she rode like a Queen.

Then, as now her promise was soon forgot,
Months turned into years, a score and ten,
The letter, full of memories, was a heartache, torture to bear,
So I hid it away, trying to forget it was there,
It was then that current operation,
The feelings of which she was unaware.
For she is the wife of a brother most dear,
And I never see him either, could not remember the year
He ever called to see me, to ask how I'd been?

And how I loved him and cried, when misfortunes hit him.
I'd brought him up when a baby, struggles too numerous to tell
And when he was at war in the Navy, sent him parcels,
Always crying, worrying through nights and days of Hell.

I wonder how *they* see these omissions in life,
Time lost forever, without happiness and rife
With sadness, and wondering why they never came along?
Always praying and hoping, I would once again belong
To two people that I loved, a brother and his wife.

God gave me our Stephen to love all my life.
Before he was born I knew,
I saw a bouncing babe, clinging to the bedpost, dangling away,
It was his first light of day,
And forever I loved him, till his last day,
As sadly now he has passed away!

HOW IT WAS

Reminiscence brooding, call it what you will,
Is a game where the mind can drink its fill
Of incidents that relate, that loom when alone,
Down the spiral of life, negotiated and born.
They paint a picture of passing time,
Coloured with happiness, sorrow, adding reticence,
Darkening the niches, hard enough to climb.

Stretched out years, with their ebb and flow,
Their trials and heartaches with no place to go.
Caught in a web, spun in anger, through hate,
Circumstances tightening the coil, the treacherous bait.

I let my love flow, ignoring the few
Sarcastic innuendoes that festered and grew
Into malicious facts, jealousy and envy the spur,
Indifference from him, and torment from her.
Pain they say, each has so much to bear,
I have had my fill, have had my share.

Death and sickness being a part,
The torturous healing that scarred the heart.
Leaving gullies of pain seeping into the soul,
To a river of anguish, with no outlet at all.
Leaden the day, no hope in the sky,
No glean from horizons that just pass by.

A mechanical being, with a heart of stone,
Automatic and doing the necessary prone
Activities and gestures to human life,
Caught in malediction of continuous strife.

Then God in his mercy answered your prayer,
Pleadingly spoken when no one was there,
As with hope you asked, now in thanks you pray
As your eyes open slowly on a bright new day.

Reminiscence will be light, you see a baby's smile,
You acquiesce omissions, and allow the style,
Of a way of life, in a narrow groove,
Allow human failings, from which you have struggled to move.

HUMAN FAILINGS

God gave us this life, on this pleasant earth,
Conceding us to use it, as we grew from birth
To love our neighbour, with reason and right,
To keep the commandments ever in sight.
We are all people, equally born to be gay,
But greed spikes man, turning good away.
Dictates differentials, a changing day.
Incites envy, with a malicious spleen,
That gains momentum, for a future scene.
Manifesting monsters, as opposed to men,
Ruthless killing, their only yen.
Who conceived this murderous sick pack,
With the craving for power to torture and ransack
This pleasant earth, this world of you and me,
With flaying fear from the Jack boot, and the shouldered gun
From a bomb, only in imagination you can see,
Cringing the hearts of humans, only wanting a start,
To live life in the span allotted to them.
With exploratory happiness, love and peace, Amen.
God gave us this life, well what went wrong?
What made a dirge, out of a beautiful song?

HUMAN NEGLECT

It clops round the back streets pulling a heavy load,
But at the end of the day, there is no warm abode,
For a wind-lashed field is its only home,
In beating rain, with nowhere to roam.
Tethered too, it spends its life,
The poor workhorse, cold, neglected, left to its strife,
Depending on humans, who are the ones so
Inhuman and heartless, leaving an animal with nowhere to go,
No stable for shelter, and then with the snow,
No food for sustenance, on the frozen ground,
With no voice for its plight, to draw attention around.
For someone's mercy, to have a heart
For a dumb animal, bereft and apart.
Hungry and cold, in incessant rain,
I ask someone, somewhere, to think again.
For my heart is broken each long winter's night,
Thinking and dwelling on this pitiful sight.
That horses thus waiting, having to stand and bear
This miserable existence. Does anyone care?

I CAN DREAM

Suppressed emotions fighting free,
Masks and faces which is me?
Walking the town, noting thereof
The concrete trends put up as mod,
Doing nothing to please, to surprise my eye,
Just uniform structures, I pass hurriedly by.
The tumult within me churning more loud,
I wanted so much, an infinity yearning, beneath a shroud.
A passing acquiescing my mobile face,
False to my mind, to all I embrace.
A mode of living, unsettled, fractious moments from another time,
Beyond this place, contours mosaic in intricate line.
Rectangular planes that ebb and flow,
Articulating people, profiles dilating, and forming slow.
As in dreams shuttling to and fro
Beckoning me the way to go.
Walking alien streets, squared and white,
Dark where greenery steals the light.
Startling in the hotchpotch twine
Of exotic blossoms heady as wine.
Dirt track roads, niched with a shelving stair,
Twix fauna and boulder, a path of rude construe,
A lure to the ocean, a thundering there.

Frothing, spewing, its timeless ode,
Under sun and moon, over smooth silver sands, its own abode.
Narrow alleyways, where footsteps weave,
Where minds collide, in lover's dreams.
So many emotions smote the heart,
Fragments of happiness, with me a part.
Secrets held for so long, eroding the soul,
Ever fighting for love's elusive goal.

I HAVE NOTHING TO WEAR

"You will have to wait, I have nothing to wear,"
The petulant voice came from the top of the stair.
Did another voice, in frustration swear and say,
"O no not again, heaven help us, not again,
With two wardrobes so full,
That to push and to pull,
Is the only way to make the door fit,
After fiddling around with the catch for a bit.
With a back room resembling a growing boutique,
Along with rows of shoes, like a centipede's den,
To match this or that,
Or kick off where or when."
The lady, still angry, is ranting again,
From the top of the stair
Comes, "I have nothing to wear,
It really is sickening,
It is always the same."
"I wish we had not said we would go out tonight,
Are you quite sure dear that you got the date right?"
The dark brown voice, really browned off now,
Booms, "You know my love, you should take a bow."
Comes the stinging answer,
With volumes to say,
Pouring out like a newsreel,
It always goes that way.
Her spouse can't win, though it was a good try,
Words somehow just pass him by.
"You think I've to wear the same old rag night and day."
"It is all right for men, but women are different so they say."
His sarcastic remark is drowned in the flow
Of exasperated phrases, unbecomingly so.

The banging of doors, with coat hangers that fall,
With the swish of a dress, rudely thrown at the wall.
"Come on now," he is trying and coaxing again,
"If this goes on we will miss Helen and Ken,
And ten to one get caught in the rain.
Surely there is something in that lot?
What is wrong with the black, or the one trimmed with Lamé,
For goodness sake, put a move on, and see what you've got!"
"Men, I am fed up with everything, so who's to blame?
I am not saying that it's you, but you are all the same."
The dark brown voice getting a word in again,
Says, "Concessions, concessions, you can say that again."
"Things go out of fashion, and when I go out,"
The lady carries on in the same old vein.
"I like to look and feel like a star,
To revel in the moment, and forget who we are.
To sweep past nosy neighbours in ermine and mink,
To drive away in a cadillac, knowing what they would think!"
Then a miraculous silence,
The spouse bored and waiting, cigar in hand,
Couldn't give a damn at whatever she has found,
Wardrobes are now silent, he does not miss the sound,
He is wishing he'd gone out, and had a round,
He longs for a drink, and wonders when and how,
Or if ever tonight he'll get one at all?
He is ready to explode and go up the wall.

When suddenly footsteps fall on the stair,
And behold a vision of loveliness is patting her hair.
Relieved she smiles; he changes the nearly said swear,
To "You have made it then,
I thought you said you had nothing to wear?"

I MUST LET YOU KNOW

I live on a terrace, very ordinary it's true,
But when the sun shines and skies are blue
I dream of walking soft sprung ground,
Where trees and flowers grow around.
Where nature's cycle has given birth
To furry creatures, birds and things
Born with the instincts of what life brings.

Flashes of silver from a lazy stream.
A meadow crimson with poppies, all part of the dream.
A mix of cowslips and wild briar rose,
Sheltering mayflowers in repose.

The dream goes on to a shady wood,
Finding ferns and bluebells with a pungent smell
Sleeping in the silence and casting a spell.
The spell of bygone days,
Of youthful ways,
Picking bouquets of bluebells to put in jars,
Innocence and happiness, with no place for wars.
Sweet recall in sweet dreams, of once upon a time,
Blessed by the sun, my inspiration to start and end in rhyme.

I WUDN'T SAY OWT

I'm glad tha's called, that tha's fon thee way,
Fer I've had summat ta say, aye fer mony a day.
How long sin I saw thee, id cant' a bin then,
Well come on in, thy aren't lookin' thee sen,
Sit in yon chair, we'll have a natter in comfort,
It's better thad way, and thy con light thy pipe, while I mek sum tay.
I woz talkin' ta Matthew only t'other day,
And con he talk, he'd plenty ta say.

It fair gi' me a shock like, whad he towd me,
So I thowt I'd sit back a bit, an' wait an' see.
Won't be a tick lad, kettle's dancin' away,
There thad's got id, now whad did I say?
Tay will cool onta t'hob a bit, while I cut some bread,
An I'll just put some jam on, then I'll hear whad tha's sed.

Course tha'll shove id down, it'll warm cockles o' thee heart,
Fer thy were fair pinched, when thy come in at start.
Fer by gum it's cowd, wudna think it woz May,
Wi them March winds blowin', I'll no be castin' no clout.
Not this week, or next, not till May is out.
Well as I woz sayin' afor I med tay,
Yon mon he'll be off again, as soon as comes neight,
An whad he gets, it'll serve him reight.

Who'd a thowt, he were thad sort, that he'd a bin sa keen,
Now don't look sa gormless, tha knows whar I mean.
Who'll lead him a ta-ta will 'yon won',
Mark me words, it'll be reight,
An' it won't be long afore she's bleedin' him white.
That's if he's any blood left, and thy could o' fooled me last neight.

Meks yer wonder what's in yon mon's brain,
Fancy, sex at his age, he must be insane!
He'll no but be fust,
An' he'll no but be last,
An' when I towd him thad he said, thy weren't as vicious as me,
Then I reight got me hair off, towd him when it was too late he'd see,
An' when thy got ta know, whar all t'others did know,
He'd be sorry he'd said owt, fer when thy were roused,
Thy sure could speak,
Not carin' who heard thee, thy ne'er woz a sneak.

He's fair gone dotty, who has him on a string has yon whore.
But as I said, it'll only lead ta his own front door.
So if thy sees him, I wudn't say owt,
Just bide thee time till he lets summat drop
Then when t' ball's rollin', give him all thy's got!
So think on whad I've towd thee, keep things ta thee sen,
An' don't let it be as long afore thy steps o'er t' mat again.
Fer if thy's owt like me, thy'll have enjoyed this chat.
And by the way I forgot ta tell thee,
He brought yon back here t'other day,
But no change did who get owt o' me I can say.

She woz ooglin' and ogling wi' her eyes,
Yon mon's going ta get such a surprise.
So remember again, I wudn't say owt, if he comes down thy way
Let him do all talkin', he'll have enough to say.
Fer he might get nasty, he's so wrapped up in yon whore,
And I'd like ta be there if owt happens, ta pick thee up from t' floor,
So thy can see thisen out now, if thy's finished thy tay.
And go easy onta handle, don't slam the door shut thy way,
And just watch thy step, if thy sees owt o' yon whore,
Fer thee and me knows what's what like,
And we're straight, though we've nowt
And it's best like I said, I wudn't say owt!

IDEAS

I can't form ideas just to suit your book,
My mind is my own, and as I take a look
At the world around, the aspect is mine,
Though the seasons do influence when the sun does shine.
Flowers and trees merge, thus inspiring rhyme.
Words just flow, a spontaneous thing,
Like the trill of a lark in early spring.

The theme comes from the immediate, or thoughts you have found
Stem from nostalgic years, that suddenly abound
From skeins of memory, flowing like a refrain,
The whole akin to an old master's beauty, restored again.
The content just fitting the moment in time,
The cocoon having burst, just manifesting in rhyme,
Stirring emotions, giving substance the whole, lilting like a song,
Ideas fashioning life, with words colourful and strong.

IMAGINATION

I imagine a primrose, delicate and pale.
I imagine a starling, does it swoop or sail
Through a morning sky, clouds billowing white,
With patches of blue, that will expand before night?
I imagine a garden, sweet in repose,
Nurturing beauty, and the scent of a rose.
I hear rustling trees as I walk neath a moon,
I imagine its face as it goes gliding by,
And as raindrops fall, I am resigned and sigh,
To sink in depression, to scream and to cry
In momentary despair, "Oh why, oh why?"
Such mundane things, earthy and true,
To eyes that see, I have learned of, only from you.

For though my eyes are open, they vacantly stare,
As the hours tick away, with no objects there.
Leaving imagination to work overtime,
With pictures looming, through ears sharp and fine,
Imagining the day as it unfolds each dawn.
Imagining romance - sensuous, warm.
Imagining the future with someone to share
Imagination and life with loving care.

IN A GARDEN

I stepped into a garden, through a creaking gate hung low
On an old stone wall, fingers of lichen splayed softly around,
Trailing mossy tendrils on the ground.
No borders here to conform to,
You just let your feet push their way through.
Towering Hollyhocks near at hand,
Courted yellow Sunflowers sheltering the spot
Where the Pansies formed a yellow band.
I gazed at a velvet upturned face,
That was speckled gold, like a pattern in lace.
Marguerites gave off a pungent smell
As they mingled with Delphiniums in that overgrown dell.
Pushing back a bramble, I smelt at a Rose,
Its fragrance intoxicating, and in its beauty did see
Floating in its aura, another me.
Beyond the haze of a silver sea, where whispering pines,
Speared tall, in the night a place of shadows and irregular lines,
Unfolded a memory, coming back
From somewhere mislaid, along the track.
She was there in a garden, with the scent of a rose,
I placed one in her hair, as she held my heart,
A beautiful garden where love did start.
But she held a secret, and we had to part.
It was the last time I saw her, and like the rose,
She was gone the very next day.
Why had I come, to lay a ghost in a garden
Of all the most appropriate places I know,
For they say in a garden
You are nearer to Heaven, than any other place
On earth you may know.

IN AN OLD BROWN CHURCH

Meandering down a leafy lane,
Inhaling the tang of the sea,
An open gate drew me off my beat
Through a tangle of weeds, to a rustic seat.
I sat speculating where I could be
In this overgrown garden,
Near the surge of the sea.

Then I knew, I had strayed onto hallowed ground,
As circling some trees an old brown church I found.
It seemed to beckon, looked so remote and forlorn,
Its weathered stance was eroded and worn.
Then the sun came out and gilded its face,
Showing such beauty, in its ageless grace.

Under its porch its door bleached with age,
Set the scene for a novel from a Bronte page.
Flashing a memory of bygone years,
Of a sorrow born with unshed tears.

I stepped out of the sun, through the gloom of the door,
Where a musk pervaded, with something more.
The air was chilly, like the dank stone floor,
And my feet sounded hollow, walking through pillars tall,
Passed a font, squared and deep,
Passed veiled-eyed statues scrolled on the wall,
To an altar, all mellow in the streaming sunlight,
From a stained glass window, blazoning down from a height.

And caught rosy red, were the faces where,
They turned saddened eyes to a Crucifix there.
Chalices of silver, and plates of gold.
Stood tarnished on a cloth, threadbare and holed.
Reflecting in this transient glory of shade,
The lustre of yesteryears, sparkled, new made.

An open missive, thumbed, yellowed and worn,
Stirred visions of Mass, marriage, death and new-born.
Of primitive rituals, captives held with scorn,
Their frightened eyes, all lost and forlorn.
What manner of men, and in what tone of voice,
Chanted its messages, without favour or choice.
Gone now forever in the sleep of time,
Do their nebulous spirits chant liturgy in mime?

Suddenly the sun was gone, and in that strange half light
The silence smote like a tolling bell,
Bringing foreboding with a dismal knell.
I brushed aside a tear as I knelt in the gloom,
Filled with turbulent emotions, in that hallowed room.

Enhanced was the moment, rising to a higher plain,
And in sincere prayers I repeated a name.
Then in a window shone a brilliant light,
The sun was shining again, it had rolled back into sight.
Touching the altar, and floor of stone
With its golden wash, as if to atone
For the moments, I had knelt with tears on my face,
Feeling inadequate, and lost in the race.

A lamp burned low, I had found the pungent smell,
So indiscreet, I could hardly tell.
Just a wisp of smoke over a chancel pew,
Unravelling the past with perception brand new.

With a last look around, for it was time to go,
An aura swamped me, I was happy and aglow.
I left the altar in a sense of calm.
With the musk mingled incense, exuding a soothing balm.

Had a miracle evolved with the sun's golden rays?
With so many mysteries, I will leave you to say.
In that old brown church something did spark,
And entered my soul, and had touched my heart
With love and fortitude, with hope all a part.
I knew now where I was going, where forever did start,
In an old brown church, yes it held my heart!

IN SUMMERTIME

A caterpillar eats another leaf,
A cricket chirps in loud relief,
Timing the bee, with its buzzing drone,
The forest's alive, a haven prone
To harbouring secrets along its verdant way,
Nature's calling night and day,
Procreating in a creature's world,
In a flurry of wings in feathery down,
A bushy tail turning seeking eyes around.
A wealth of growing, in a weaving of time,
Living, evolving like a rainbow, in natural rhyme.
A bee and a flower condoning the code,
A Jackdaw cawing, in a different mode
Of summer madness, the cycle won't wait,
Trees swathing in their greenery,
Dappling coins of gold
On meadows and hedgerows, and paths over the wold.
A babbling brook, meandering at will
In the summer sun to an old water mill
Rotating mechanically, its wheel clear cut and clean,
Its droplets dancing in the frothy scene
Flourishing the wild rose, its face tinged red,
Its vines a-trailing the water's rough stony bed.
Oh maturing summer, running true to form,
Natural beauty in glorious adorn
Your poignant aura, your meadows of hay,
Your mellowing of emotions at the end of the day.
A time for everyone, human nature blending in rhyme
In summertime.

INVOLVEMENT

Life's an involvement, a tangible thing,
Loving, breathing, wanting to give, and the emotions they bring.
Impulses, yearnings, flutter the heart,
Ending in dreams.
God's in his heaven as we pass by dimensions apart,
Straddling humanity over vistas wide,
Piercing the soul with beauty men see,
The intricate weave,
Destined for you and me.
Weeding the paths to bequeath his seed
In Nature's wilderness to fruition, with the good of the deed.
Teeming wildlife, a picturesque scene,
To cull or let go this benevolent flow.
Ever seeking, ever hoping, the winds of change will blow
Revelations asleep, cocooned in the brain
Peak like quicksilver, they unwind so slow,
But are prone to musings to the familiar that we know.
I look to the mountains, to the sky, or a tree,
All God's creations to assess, to see
On a sun-drenched beach, breakers rolling free.
You can take your pick, as likewise me.
Involvement free
Questions to answer, the agenda simple happiness in life,
So let it be!

I'VE TA BAKE A CAKE

I've ta bake a cake, but other things on me mind
Have thrown me late, fer things o' that kind.
I've bin through shoppin', supermarkets an' all,
Comparing prices, hopin' they'd fall.
But every week, they've just gone up,
An' it's same wi' t' drink, an' we've nowt ta sup.
An' comin' Christmas, murder there'll be,
An' I'd much rather it woz you than me.
All shops are plastered, wi' how much off fer a litre,
Fer a dozen, save on a quart,
Meks yer wonder if after all, horse comes before t' cart.
So besides lookin' fer currants, an' raisins too.
I have to traipse ta th'off licence, an' by gum there's a few.
Fer Burnley's well known fer wettin' th'head
At births an' funerals, an' when folks get wed.

We'd a reight owd do when our Tommy woz born,
Or so I woz told, fer I woz left on me own
In yon fancy hospital, they call it Bank Hall,
Listenin' ta a lot o' kids scrikin', sendin' me half up t' wall.
But rantin' on won't bake me a cake,
So I'll have ta geet crackin' afore it's too late.

So all th'ingredients, I'll scribble on a list,
Then nip round selling owt shop, fer all I've missed,
Like whisky an' t' gin, an' a few crates o' beer,
I'll have ta get bottles in, to help wi' t' good cheer.
Fer who the heck wants a cake
Wi' no wallop ta take?
I'd ne'er live it down, me name 'ud be mud
Wi' me husband, bakin' a cake fer Christmas wi' no beer,
And no whisky's no good, no no fear!

JACK FROST

Frost had patterned the windowpane,
Capturing condensation that had dribbled like rain.
Now an elegant sheet, a silvered flow
Of delicate tracery, an artistic show.
A winter wonderland had invaded my room,
As huddled in bed, I scanned out at the gloom.
Frosty fingers had fashioned crimps and scallops, deftly wove,
Ruched three dimensionally, spraying out to behove
A feathery landscape, pristine white,
With a freezing sparkle chilling the night.
Chilling also my brain, its concentration of whatever might
The morning hours bring into sight
Of the world outside, taking the measure of this view,
This fairyland, so deceptive too!
Would I manage to walk, even stand on my feet,
If frozen snow was swathing the street?
A pretty scene on a postcard, nostalgic and clean,
Bringing childhood memories happy and serene.
Waiting for Christmas,
Building a snowman with smoky candles agleam,
Stuck down in a jar, tied and looped around, and held up by string.
As from door to door in the night,
Off-key carols we did sing.
Jack Frost was a friend then in them days of yore,
His frozen touch never cold, as we skid and slid on the floor.
Now it all seems so far away; when did my options find a new range?
I abhor such activities, just how long since the change?
Is it age, common sense, or just plain rage
That when the temperature plummets, and deems to let in
This long ago friend, now definitely no kith or kin,
I resignedly shudder at windows frosted like lace,
And burrow deeper into my pillow, the bedclothes covering my face.

111

JUST A CORNER OF SPAIN

Just a corner of Spain, mine for a time,
An effervescent sojourn I think of in rhyme.
Hotels of concrete doing nothing to deter
From arabesque beauty, and sounds the sea does incur.
Breakers screaming ever to be free, spewing over golden sands,
Eroding footsteps in irregular bands.
Eternal vigilance from a mountain's grey stone,
A backdrop of majesty, proud and prone
To swapping secrets with wind and rain,
At the moment zero, with suspect disdain.
The in thing being the sun, beaming in style,
Conjuring spectres of tranquillity in a forest of pine.
Tempting me to walk its way, to traverse its depths of cool shade,
Where fantasies loom, and spells pervade.
White painted ironwork, a filigree of lace,
Twining with vines from a green leafy base.
Whose hand did fashion, did leave this trace
Of a once loved house, with a neglected face,
With a lemon tree shading a windowpane,
Where a wilting geranium cried out for rain.
Flowers weeding, creeping once a riot to enhance
A forgotten garden, forever in stance.
A poignant scene to fold in memory, nostalgic, mine,
Just a corner of Spain to imbue in time,
Blending yearnings for youth to dance, to belong,
To be part of this land of Spanish song.
Its fascinating aura, its carefree high,
Showering flamenco music, magic in its swift pass by,
Leaving imprints of sunshine, feather duster palms in the sky.
Treasured emotions you swear will not die in vain.
Inevitably their passing yesterday's romance to let go but not wane.

JUST LETTING YOU KNOW

I write because I am lonely, with too many hours in the day.
Decisions looming are monstrous, with no one else to say
Anything about anything, in any old way.
To talk over issues, to suggest an alternative view,
To ease the onus resting on you.

Weakness of will sullies the mind,
But body and soul must survive, and a smile is kind.
Relativity swamps the world,
But in a silent room, only ghosts relate, voiceless, unfurled.
Initiative dwindles in the singular state,
Wallowing prone, over a long ago date.

Everybody needs somebody, everyone has a place,
Love lost whenever, confusing the race.
The race for survival, struggling to form
Personal contacts, a private norm.
Those yearnings for someone, shackled with pride,
Die on confrontation, letting dreams bide.

So I write when adrenaline decides to flow,
To alleviate the hours that only the lonely know.
Not over superlative, or cleverly defined,
Just words from the heart, from thoughts more inclined
To happiness and laughter, to be one of a part
Of a band of people, would do for a start.

JUST ONE OF THOSE THINGS

A dawn wind blowing, buffeting, streaming my hair,
As taut as the emotions flooding my mind, and festering there.
My spirits were zero, would that they could fly
Like the fingers of colour, streaking the sky.
Rising, expanding to a rosy haze of light,
Banishing the grey sombre remnants of night.

Nature's cycle, as always the way,
Life goes on from this start to a beautiful day.
Prisms of gold filtered a woodland glade,
Bringing memories of love, of vows new-made.
But in another place, another time,
In a world apart, he was mine.

The horizon lit with a myriad glints, over a sea
Of dreams, fluid and free.
Just a boy and a girl planning how life should be,
Where the sun reflects in its zenith, in its quenching low,
Making way for the moonlight, and our happiness to grow.

Has this ever related to you?
Just an ordinary incident, simple but true.
Brief was the interlude, the elements grew cold.
What had changed our love; it was suddenly old,
The tumult was spent, the dreams were gone,
And only etiquette made us carry on.

Hold back the night,
Close my mind, freeze tortured thoughts that put sleep to flight.
I walk alone in this risen dawn,
Expectancy stalking me, a willing pawn

Sensing in the solitude around
A spiritual presence, soothing and tangible on the soft sprung ground.
The wind had gentled under the sun's golden ray,
So impassive now I embraced this new day,
The fetters were slipping, were dropping away,
And the culminating depths seemed now at bay,
No more would I wish my life away,

Crying for oblivion in deep, deep sleep,
Or wallowing in nostalgia as misery did creep.
For counting the cost I had come out free,
My time was now, I was alive, and once again me.
A sigh died on my lips, I drew in sweet morning air,
Seeing the golden sun, and everything there.

From a rustling tree dappling the ground,
To a cascade of water finding level ground.
Had they *always* been there, had it always been so?
In the aeons of years, I had been too blind to know.
So enmeshed in self pity, in fathoms of hate,
Straining at bonds, created for bait.

Answering questions churning my brain,
Whys and wherefores awaiting, always the same.
With this dawn streamed a happiness
I was blessed to see,
Briefly construing what will be will be,
Yes a new beginning had risen with this dawn for me,
Just one of those things, where a revelation had set me free.

KNOWLEDGE

Rivers of knowledge flow in subtle subterfuge,
Spawning in devious minds
A wielding power with the ultimate find.
Cosmic waves spark a theoretical fuse,
Nebulous, shadowy, drifting in space,
With a transient aura, involving your soul,
Waiting trance-like, for a receptive call.

Strange emotions that carry you away,
Beyond the Universe where night and day
Merge in a backdrop of irrelevant time,
Beyond all reason, beyond all rhyme.
Tumult streaked with terror, stirs your brain,
Releasing yearnings so profound, your thoughts seem insane,
As they float you out into a timeless void,
Through a purple swathe, forever afar,
Through a myriad glints that exude from a star.

Mystical galaxies harbouring love and hate,
With visions of what will be will be,
Power and greed, destruction, wars depicted in blood,
With Nemesis pointing a finger at me.
Iridescent colours forming a protective cloak,
Serrating the darkening folds of grey
Show approaches golden, a stairway to a golden day.
For the lone traveller, though the phenomenon be fey,
It speaks of magic doing things to the heart,
Revealing, all revealing, tearing you apart
Like quicksilver shifting, whilst creeping, piercing your soul,
O where, O where, in this deep is your goal?

Past moon and stars now, it is the witching hour,
Where more hate than love does thrive and shower
From mystic spells flashing from space,
To make or mar the Human Race.

Drifting in realms of an enchanted night,
Bringing knowledge for wrong or right.
Nurtured seeds lying dormant, stir,
To blossom in the magic, that these hours incur.
Will they bring forth love, stem an errant heart
Or overgrown with seeds of hate, strangle growth in the dark?
Or have they festered too long in stagnant pools,
Where crystal waters have mulled dank and green,
Seething with violence, greed and hate,
Whilst shimmering with that treacherous sheen,
Float with a skim, a subterfuge bait.

Pools of iniquity empty and flow,
The golden staircase beckons, and up I must go,
Letting the seeds of hate into infinity blow.
Struggling emotions, calm at the call
Of heavenly forces that converge over all.
Mystery, fantasy, have you had your fill,
The moment is yours to ponder at will.
A path is swept with a steady beam,
Challenging your reason; are things as you deem?
The unfolded panorama, a beautiful scene.

Where time is forever, with a smile on its face,
A gossamer world, shimmering in truth and grace.
Where all is revealed from the mystic urge,
Where knowledge breeds love, and hate is drowned with a dirge.

LET IT BE

A world of dreams awash in my brain,
Waves of nostalgia spewing in the refrain.
A haunting melody of another day,
From a sea of memories buried fathoms away.
Locked for aeons of forgotten time,
In a dormant cocoon, that had awaited this moment to evolve as mine
To relate to my life, to my heart, my soul,
To rekindle love, to find pondering, the hoped for goal.
A restricted view, an unheeded call, human failings destroying all.
Erupted emotions, impetuous and strong,
A mad concept of right and wrong
Broke the pattern, the transient time
Of love's young dream, tender and fine.
Pushing it back to a mundane thing
Pride and vanity being the bell tolled in arrogance, the mode to ring.
What did it matter, a broken heart,
The world was wide with a lifetime's start,
For drifters to gather, a stable veneer,
To cover the memories, the dirge of fear.
Just like dreams now, memories flow,
Time has mellowed the heart, for life to run more slow,
To acquiesce, to concede, these memories true
With yearnings for love once more with you.

LET THERE BE JOY

Joy intangible, can touch your heart,
Happiness how transient can be a part,
Of foolish quarrels, urging instincts for right,
As expedience and fright invade the shadows of the night.
New concepts tormenting, for what might have been,
Bring yearnings for happiness, to let go the fight.

Each waking morn, thoughts raw,
Hatred dominant, joy had nowhere to go.
What veered the mind, in this melée strong,
Of tumultuous emotions, what went wrong?
With love to abhor such a senseless stream
Of incidents, where you judged as Queen.
Vicious controversy full of urge,
Voicing innuendoes with a spiteful splurge.

Where is the joy in being this way,
Where is the happiness of yesterday?
Please God let it happen this change of heart,
Let it be sincere, an ongoing part
Of fighting for joy in people to start,
Let all this happiness, this joy to be free
Of doubt, of hatred, love and kindness, the essence of joy from me.

LIVING

My riveted gaze at a picture there made the sound of silence more hard to bear. Nostalgic threads were forming a weave of a thousand memories, I was prone to cleave. I must shed living in this aura so profound. I close my eyes then turn around willing the immediate, the mundane, to see and shake me out of this reverie. The sun is shining, the wind blows free, carrying birdsong from a nearby tree. Laughter, voices, echo nearby; it is a beautiful day neath a cloudless sky.

I saunter out and stand at the gate, and with mixed feelings I view the scene so thronged, each to his own, the pace won't wait, for it's tangled in love intrigue and hate. With no turning back each cog of the wheel gaining momentum, revolving with speed, fitting precisely each manouvred deal. Feeling lost I paused, suspended there, washed with inertia that would take me nowhere.

Inside again, I see an empty chair. How long ago did someone loved sit there? The books that are gathering dust seem to be of no consequence now, those days had gone when they had been a must, like the hands that had treasured and flicked the leaves. I was alone in a house that had once been a home, caught in a void that silence weaves.

The clock on the wall ticked the hours away, slowly but surely, bringing night and day, and the memories of what had now faded away. Fluid thoughts that flood, I try to quell the race, then the chores of a lifetime take their place. I memorise the tasks that I have tried hard to mask, and think, "I should really start to paint," but it is at this point my heart grows feint.

I walk into the kitchen, cup and plate in hand, then I'm off again thinking of when it had been different and grand. I wash up the pots, then put them to stack, wipe round the cooker till I'm spent and slack. Ah well, I decide it is out I will go, and be part of the flotsam in the world's ebb and flow. Walk on till my feet tread fields of green, to find another me, near a rippling stream. To watch tall trees sway, with the rustle of leaves, the ground's all dappled, peeping out like lace, with smatterings of daisies tinged red in the face. And I know of a copse that struggles close by, where bluebells are growing, lush and high, sweet in repose with a pungent smell, like gossamer wings each dainty bell. Such a gathering of beauty, I walk the dell, emotions stir along the way as I let my feet stray.

Suddenly my heart is light with a happy flow, emotions are rising, letting nostalgia go. The wonder of nature has stirred my will, and my eyes swivel in awareness to the rise of the hill. I feel I belong, I'm a part of all this, under the wind and the sun, with its warming kiss. The melancholia is surely no longer there, I walk home at peace, without a care, though my house is the same, still silent, still bare, with the clock on the wall ticking away. Perpetual motion it seems to say, with life having only so much time, the emphasis still there in its mellow chime, recalling again time so coloured with strife, where a tender smile was a joy in the nightmares of a bottomless pit, hoping for revelations to make your life fit into each lonely day. The same for how many, well who can say?

Whatever your sphere you walk, you breathe, with feelings, emotions, we are all bequeathed with their rise and fall that cry out and call, in the struggle against fate to carry us onto our ultimate goal. Before extinction leaves us flat, to carry on with living, a compensation, a thanksgiving, conquering all that.

MOMENTS OUT OF TIME

The silence pressed around,
I breathed in an aura, in a swathe of sound,
In a strange dimension, on grassy ground.
Trees cloaked in mystery, swayed in the winds passing by.
Woodland creatures related,
Birds celestial flapped their wings in the sky
Dominating the orb of a full-blown moon,
A susceptible lure to a stairway of doom,
A phenomenon of magic taking me high,
In transient time, in bursting rapture, a heart benign.
A swirl of euphoria, excitement aflame,
Emotions came flooding, too elusive to name.
Belonging in body, mind and soul,
An affinity of spirit twining a will-o-the-wisp call.

My future evolved into the moonlit night,
In the silence, in the yearning to be free,
To take the blazing stairway, as an invite to me.
Behind the veil the purple shroud,
Where love belongs, where beings dance and sing,
Where laughter cascades from soft to loud,
A melodious ringing in this silent sound of all fulfilment,
I was high off the ground.
Beautiful moments on wings of time,
Shimmerings of life, the mystic all mine.

A sphere of loving, of yearnings, of woven schemes,
The ebb inevitable, dissolving all, taking away dreams.
In the fauna's flurry some creature did invoke
The silence was gone, the immediate spoke,
Clearly I saw the man in the moon,
All around mundane, the spell was broke!

MY FAVOURITE BROWN

Brown is so pretty, it's what my eyes see,
Other colours I love, but it is brown for me.
I walk through a wood, neath the blue of the sky
Filtering through greenery swaying on high.
A splayed out profusion, with a rustling sound,
But my eyes just probe on from where they abound,
To the bole with its bark,
Each limb richly dark,
Swaying around
In my favourite brown.
Its girth covered in lichen, widening down
To ferns, touching stones on the earth's rich brown.
Nature nurtured from the beginning of time,
Roots and trunk growing strong to its crown.
A tree in splendour, naturally part of my favourite brown.

Daffodils slowly open their golden frill,
Flaunting their beauty on air cold and chill,
Taking stance in fickle April, behind the wooded gown,
Behind the bark of an oak,
A foil for each other, one my favourite browns.
As with the interest on occasions of shopping galore,
Escalators taking you from floor to floor.
Eventually flagging enough, enough and no more,
The tramping for you is over, it's now the nearest door.

To hit the road, get out of this town,
Away from the rummaging, the trying on,
And the putting things down.
But your eyes automatically see a display on the floor,
Streaming tinsel, and a most unusual decor.
The sight pleased my eye, banishing my frown,
The sojourn after all, had been well worth the while.
As I noticed the cut, admiring the style
Elegant and chic was the model's gown.
It had made my day; it was my favourite brown.

MY FIRST FAIRY TALE

Once upon a time there was a land called America, miles and miles away over a rolling sea, and to us children just a fairy tale. So in between the matinée sing-song, where the words of a song, were followed by a white ball bouncing upon every word, whilst a lady in a box at the side played the music on an organ, and then after the news was a caption of marching Jack Boots, row after row of news was where the precision helmeted men, with sabre and gun carried over their right shoulders, all served to make us children shudder. However it was all soon forgotten when our favourite films got underway.

Adolf Menjo, Raymond Navarro, Eddie Cantor, Gloria Swanson, Laurel and Hardy, were some of the celluloid stars of our day. But one name always sticks in my memory, for we liked the cowboys and Indians the best. It was Yakima Canute, and he was in the *'Santa-fe-Trail'*.

I was in another world that I could only dream about, and for a short spell, my imagination ran riot, and I was wrapped in this fairy tale of my dreams. I recall *'America and the Painted Desert'*, with William Boyd.

This showed places of fascination that were so different from our own hum-drum Lancashire town. Their magic lulled the dross away, as well as the doubt that such places ever existed, and as the oceans rolled, so did our dreams.

Soon childhood days were left behind us, and the hard realities of deprivation gained momentum, and showed the way, as did the brief memories of the silver screen, overshadowed now by the marching Jack Boots, men with sabre and gun, the very same ones that had spoiled our fairy tale time, and a little girl's dream, and fascination with America, and for Yakima Canute.

But you see fairy tales can come true, for I have now been to America, with the sweet nostalgia of childhood memories ever fresh, with the happiness that the cinema once brought to me. I was not disappointed!

MY LIVING FIRE

My living fire in my lonely room.
Cheers my life chasing the gloom
Not only from around me,
But within my heart, for in its glow, pictures I see,
A spiral of memories tumble free.

Emotions stir, and within me loom,
Spirits that fuse in the fire's glow,
With the flickering shapes that spurt and zoom,
Chasing the shadows on the wall,
With darts of crimson that devour the coal.

Heightening the smile on a portrait there,
Whilst gilding the fall on a lock of hair.
The flames dance higher, they hiss and spume,
Lending beauty to my room.

The piano's keyboard touched with mellow light,
Brings poignant memories into sight,
Striking a chord, as a gentle flow
Of music surrounds me, that I used to know.

Young lovers are dancing in the fire's flames,
Symmetrically swaying with laughter,
Clear as a bell, I watch with rapture,
And voice their names.

Perpetual motion, dancing out of the past,
If only it was real, and could but last.
My fire lends magic, it casts a spell,
Pulling me out of my lonely hell.

But now the climax is waning, its energy spent,
The music is fading with a glow that lent
A flash of memory to invade my room,
From the heart of the fire in the oncoming gloom.

Nostalgia is around me, but I must let go,
Sufficient the moment, I let the aura flow,
And drifting thoughts push out of sight,
As I leave my fire and say, "Goodnight."

MY TAPESTRY

A forced stay in bed, nothing much to do or say,
My veranda window looked out over a bay,
But my bed did not lay
Parallel with the view,
Spoiling my visions of the going's on of the day.
So I sighed and tried to read, but just stared ahead
At the grey wall stippled white,
Longing for sleep, that I knew wouldn't come before night.

Resigned I lay there, propped up so,
When my gaze was arrested, did a vision flow?
Yes, I was suddenly aware
A tapestry was forming in front of me there,
And thus immobile I enjoyed the surprise,
As figures danced before my eyes.

Scenes and things popped up at will,
Stretching from the door to the windowsill.
Amidst flurries of snow
Was a stark mountain range,
With a bedraggled army, deflated and slow,
Travelling wearily each curve and bend,
Hoping for somewhere which would lend
Shelter, and respite, to lick clean its wounds,
Rekindle its spirit, in its cavern-like tombs.

Mayday was obvious, with maypoles, stalls, and a Big Top,
With a tumbler juggling, to make the crowds stop.
Knights on white chargers, went galloping by,
With silvered lances and swords at their thigh.
Who was the villain, and where was the place
He would be destined to die?

A peacock strutting throws his head up high,
As a gaggle of geese go waddling by.
A waving cornfield with the sun up high,
Spotted red with poppies, such beauty I sigh!
A sparrow sways on a bursting rose,
Near a solitary lighthouse weathered in repose.

A forest glade shot with golden light,
Dapples swans on a river, drifting elegant and white.
With the river flowing on over boulders and stones.
A willow tree bows low, as if to atone
For deeds committed at the water's rim,
Whilst a recycled moon rolls gently in.

A mossy bank rises high to a ledge,
Where a crumbling tower and fortress wall,
Are scattered with lichen, rose briar softening its edge.
Wizards and fairies casting spells,
Fly from turrets of castles ringing with bells
To catch hobgoblins, and light the fuse,
That will burn all witches there around,
From wooden pyres piled high from the ground.

Coats of arms, lions and unicorns are there,
And even a griffin with a certain flair,
Mix with gargoyles as trumpets sound,
Blown by heralds in red and gold,
Proclaiming amnesty over the wold.

Tubs of flowers sit on an old stone wall,
A poacher out shooting, his prey it does fall.
Strings of dancers, light as air,
Their flowing movements depicted there.

Sporting sashes of green, and Scotch kilts too,
Mingling with ribbons of red, white and blue.
With thistles and roses strewn all around.
A scattering of daffodils, and a very large leek,
While an old woolly ram saunters, subdued and meek.

Majestic conifers pierce the sky,
With a lone heron flopping by,
Blazing a trail to the hump-backed bridge,
Before discreetly dropping, over a ridge.

Further along a sandpiper glides,
Where cooing lovebirds manoeuvre free
Seeking their haven in a cherry tree.
Bob-tailed rabbits frolic and play,
Forming a circle to end the day.

Then a glorious sunset gilds my room,
Its crimson face a piercing the gloom
Of grey fingers a streaking by,
With a vermilion thrust, lighting the sky.
Stretching a ladder of silver across the sea,
And through my window in the quickening night,
I know that it did it just for me.
To catch my tapestry on the wall,
Its shafts of light embracing all.

They say spells are cast out there in the gloom,
After sunset and beneath the moon,
But magic had worked another spell,
Timing this tapestry I have recorded so well,
To break the monotony of my day,
And the sun has blessed it with its dying rays.
Who says God does not work in mysterious ways?

MY WORLD

Passing through my mind was a wave of despondent thought. There was nothing of interest on TV today, for sport to me was a zero. I could stand Jim Davidson, for he helped the game along, so it was only snooker in small doses. But game shows like chat shows bored me out of my mind. All that hullabaloo, the voices, and posturing for attention were not my kind of viewing.

I longed for discovery, for the drama of mystery that could be talked over underneath a welcomed thatch, an old inviting hearth of stone, smoke-blackened with the fires of many years, and the traveller lulled into its warm embrace.

Truth or fiction, human life was the pivot relived in a story told by a fireside, to question, to mesmerise the bored mind. Ah well each to his own. I switched onto Channel Two.

I know now that it was a film, *'The Last Elephant'*, and something urged me to watch, and soon I liked what I saw. But not for long, for elephants were being shot and maimed, with a girl caught up in the destruction of the scene. I knew that such practices were prevalent in Africa and India, but I was heartbroken and terribly disturbed by the slaughter.

I watched through to the ultimate end, sorrow and satisfaction at the outcome fitting into place, as a glance at my paper stated it to be a film. The content was sad, for I strongly deplore any form of cruelty to God's creatures, but I would ask the powers that be to show more of the same, together with the kindness of so many people who spend their time and money on sick animals, for animals have no voices of their own.

What sort of a human being can starve and hurt a dumb animal? I love Rolf Harris and Pet Rescue. Please let us have more such programmes, for they are loved and appreciated by viewers like me. I know that always more money is needed for the RSPCA, and they do such a worthwhile job that I like to help them in any way that I can.

NANCY'S ROOM

Bunnies, Jumbos, Mickey Mouse too,
All cuddly and furry, to mention a few.
A fabulous ice-cone, with cherry on top,
Streaming raspberry in its elegant pot.
A checkout till, standing silent near the wall,
Tops the roll of a precariously placed nursery ball.
Paddington in a cot, a brush and comb near the bath
Left on the lawn, and straddling the path
To a white painted doll's house,
With a red and yellow splash.
And a cot overflowing with numerous dolls,
Jessica, Pricilla, Mindy and Mayne,
Their sightless eyes waiting, the pretending game,
For the make-believe hour, with its magic spell
When Nancy gets busy, then who can tell
In the world of a child what adventures do loom,
What happiness ensues in that toy-filled room?
The boy under the lamp, jumps clear and free,
Helping the shell lady down, to join in the spree.
They say "Hello" to Nancy for the time is just right,
To hide from the lion, that stalks into sight.
So it is into the doll's house, to plan and make tea
For Miss Piggy and Kermit will be guests you see.
A lady in a costume will be the host,
With a confederate soldier the last,
But the most honoured guest.
Nancy's planned it just so,
See he walks up the path with his lady in tow.

They all drink a toast, and chatter away,
Then Creme Puff, the dog stands,
Commanding all eyes his way,
Saying, "The lion is lonely, and all he wants is to play,
Shall we invite him to join us,
And do you all agree with what I say?"
"Yes," said Nancy, "It will be just fine,
I have always fancied a lion, as a playmate of mine.
And as the theatre is quite handy, only a few steps away,
Let us surprise him, and make his day,
To hear the muppets sing, their round-de-lay.
Look Grandad's beckoning Miss Piggy,
To slip into the show,
And Kermit will supervise, to make it all go.
Jack and Jill, the Indians will dance what they know,
Their waving and stamping, will add to the din,
And if we all hurry, we can then join in.
See Carie the elephant is leading the way,
So come on everybody, it's a wonderful day!"

Please note:
Creme Puff is a brown dog with a long creme ear.
And the tree in the backyard, blossomed this year.

NATURAL THINGS

Floating clouds cover half the sky,
And a patch of blue goes racing by.
The wings of swallows join the flight
To rest and wait for the coming night.
A woodpecker pecks, with a swift intent,
And is watched by the woodman on his bent.
Shivering trees start a rustling tune,
While lovers hope for a silvery moon.
Then a beaver breaks the water's calm,
A gentle ripple where it's safe from harm.
A splash is felt, clouds run true to form,
Hurrying groups of people on their way,
Casting anxious eyes towards the sky,
Hoping to beat the gathering storm
That has chased all beauty from their day.
The wind is roused, it eddy's and turns,
Whipping their bodies, while their faces it burns.
The sky grows dark, and the woodpecker's gone,
And the silence comes crowding on.
You are the last of the group as you leave nature behind
For the noise of the city, to be alone there with its kind,
Where the sky, if it's grey goes unnoticed here,
And the rain only fills the hotels for its beer.
Where a rustle of leaves is never heard,
Nor a thought given to the song of a bird.

Well later maybe, will out come the moon,
And someone, somewhere, will walk quite soon
On the soft-trodden earth neath a rustling tree
Hopefully me!
Then with someone we love, all nature around,
We will love, and be loved, truly thankful of all found
Content with nature far into the night,
Sleep will make everything right.

NO MORE, NO MORE!

Awake as usual, a restless night,
With thoughts and fancies all put to flight.
Wide awake now, it was too late to care,
And someone was abroad in the cold morning air.

Clattering clog irons on wet paving stones,
Clinched the reality I knew in my bones.
It was Sam off to work, I might have known the clock would win,
And the time was now, when I heard that din!

No alarm clock was needed when Sam did his stint
Of steps in staccato, as of clog irons on flint.
I banished all thoughts of more sleep for that day,
As the clatter of Sam's clogs slowly faded away.

It was six o'clock on a wet windy morn,
I shivered as I dressed, wishing I'd never been born.
Downstairs now, I made breakfast for four,
Turning from the cooker, I saw all the clogs shining by the door.

The sight of those clogs sparked a memory flow,
As the bacon I turned, then the gas jet down low.
It broke through the cobwebs of sleep in my brain,
Trance-like I stared brushing threatening tears about to flow like rain

Denoting your class it was always clogs down our way,
And my dad, like Sam, had to clatter over flags
And cobbles to earn a living at the mill,
And I had to work there, like I have to do still.

No back doors to a ladder of fame,
Just hardworking folk, gradely and game.
And there are so many memories and tales I could tell,
Where in glimpses of heaven, I left this man-made hell.
Left all the squalor and my clogs behind,
Far away from Sam's clogs and the daily grind.

God let it happen, and for those who seek, find!
A place, a home, of a far removed kind
You can be proud of, and admire with a pleasing decor,
But please don't let there be anymore
Clogs that need blacking, to be polished by me.
Any more blinking clogs standing shiny on the floor,
To clatter away your life, waiting outside the door.

OBSERVING ALL

Swaying trees, rustling leaves,
A whispering wind giving gentle heaves
To the splay of greenery, high
Etched in the changing, darkening sky.
A flight of birds winging home
Broke the solitude with their flapping drone.
A lone bird, a straggler, swift in their wake,
Blazoning a trail for its errant mate.
In exuding moon glow,
Glowing bright, ghosting in the surge and flow
Of drifting shadows, now a deeper hue,
Claiming the light, the summer's blue.
Swathing purple fusing the grey,
Time the essence, having its say.
Making the moment, frittering sanity away,
Leaving the world, this sheltered glade
To the witching hour, where dreams are made,
Mixed with visions, airy, fey,
Being near tangible this time of day.
Suspended emotions that surely lend
A soothing reverie in a gilded night,
Flashing magic in a shower of moonlight,
Observing still that golden sphere,
Living a drama, each detail so clear,
That momentarily quenching the moon into cloud,
The actors still dance so poignantly their shroud.
Solitude the vessel, deep as the sea,
Brimming with memories and dreams that be
The future, the past, this moment, this night,
Rolling in fantasy, in enchanted moonlight.
Quickening the mind, observing all,
Wrapping a piece of life into a magic ball.

ONCE UPON A TIME OF DAY

Memories so tangible, that I want to cry
As pictures dance before my eyes.
Once I belonged, was part of the scene,
Full of everything life had been.
The child held a bun with ice on top,
As the strap-book marked the date and a penny
As she ran from the shop
Hoping the fire had kindled, and there was a brew
From a boiling kettle, and tea for two.
My little brother, less fretful, his ice-bun in lieu
Of burnt toast and dripping, our breakfast on cue
Where stone floors, and black-leading were all in a day
Of mopping, and polishing the Lancashire way.
Without even a rug on the white-stoned floor
We cadged old clothes, cut and pegged through a sugar bag
Matching colours a pleasure, to do more, to have a warm floor.
Neighbours were friends, their troubles yours,
Allowing the gossip that lightened the daily chores.
Work was something treasured like gold,
By those that were young, those grown prematurely old.
The General strike of the Twenties, hitting all around,
Weavers and Pit-workers, with their hopes on the ground.
Dreams set at zero, only time would conquer what we found,
As life's furrow we ploughed, making the fold
To cover destiny's mark of dross to gold.
Memories so tangible, tears fall and why
I thank God for seeing all these things,
Through tears, happiness, the ultimate memory it brings
Never, oh never to pass me by.

ONLY AN INDIAN

A lake shining silver, a panorama of pines,
In verdant profusion, in forever lines.
A spiral of smoke, wigwams bright,
Chanting wails filling the sky, the night.
Tom-toms resonant, significant, drifting high,
Begging the question, will trouble be negative to fizzle and die?

A paddling canoe stops, and banks on the shore,
A dark-skinned warrior silently pads over a needle-strewn floor.
Moccasin shod, banded over the eye, garbed in soft-thonged skins
Emitting a jingle from symbolic tribal wins.
To the heart of the sound, to the beat of the drum,
What emotions stir behind the passive face?
As over to the powwow he greets his kin, his race,
Refreshed round the campfire, may it ever burn,
Swapping confidences, wisdom exuding from a mighty chief,
To a son, all evil to spurn.

Judgements gleaned from the moon and stars, heard in the wind,
In the flurry of a leaf, infallible beliefs never to rescind.
Fulfilling destinies fated long ago, the world alien, knowledge a part
Of turbulent decisions locked in the heart.

The lonesome pine, the lonesome trail,
The sun and moon's mysteries behind a shadowy veil.
An animal of nature, tracking, reading signs,
Instincts for living without a nickel or a dime.
Happy and sensuous in the rays of the sun,
Secrets harboured in warm sprung ground,
The surge of life concealed around.

Stirring the habitat of beaver and bear,
Trapping and sleeping, time irrelevant, no longer there.
Watching days grow short, with a frost-spiked moon,
With howling winds, bringing in too soon
Momentous gusts and blizzards of snow,
Where a jackal's bay joins the winter's dirge,
Hunger and pain, all emotions that flow.

Interior probes do not pass him by,
Friend or foe, he has to know why
Battling with his soul, he's learned to cope with hate,
An ancestral legacy, deceived, hunted with a treacherous bait.

Formidable the forest now in virgin snow,
The need for survival, his to know
Where men had perished, fate to him is kind,
By the frozen lake, a respite he will find.
Gathering sustenance for the long cold night,
Awaiting the whatever, and the cold morning light.

Thoughts veering to the homeward trail,
The end in sight, with his mission done in sweet prevail,
The circle slowly closing, instinctively round to those held dear,
A distant drum, a treble zero of fear.
His pack now light a warrior knows his part is done,
And the immediate sparkles with the winter sun,
Heightening the smile of a waiting squaw,
And an old man, full of thanks, for peace, not war!
Knowing his time has come, his span nearly done,
But what a glorious fight, verbally had been won.
And new life would now flow, with the look on each face,
Of 'White Cloud', and the wanderer, his only son,
Who though only an Indian, had the measure, the pace,
Of coping with prejudice, the curse of the human race.

ONLY A PHOTOGRAPH

I have only a photograph taken years ago,
To rest my eyes on, when feeling low.
Three small faces smiling, and sitting in a row.
Zoe and Alison held by David, carefully so,
Near a plant pot, in a backyard, leaves a splayed and a flow,
I imagine how they look now, and do not know.
And how many smiles from tiny lips puckered in a bow
Have I missed, on three faces as nature had them grow
Into womanhood, and manhood,
From this photograph taken years ago?
Somewhere they live and walk under God's sky,
But when imagination runs riot, I sit there and cry
For three smiling faces; someone took away,
Took my lovely grandchildren, I think of today.
When alone in a room with memories that flow,
With questions but no answers going round in a vortex,
Always as ever, yes always in tow.
As I look at the photograph taken years ago
Of three small faces, I still want to cry,
And can only pray God to bless them, until I die.

POETRY

Poetry satisfies my searching heart,
Appeasing obscurity, proclaiming a world apart,
In the ordinary everyday, run of the mill,
It creates thoughts of love, moulds my mind to its will.
Brings dreams and fancies from my awakened brain,
Gives ideas and words, a beautiful blending refrain,
That unwinds like a melody, vibrating my soul,
Ringing out with nostalgia, as memories rise then fall.
Yes poetry is the essence, dripping fluid and free,
Creating a heavenly day, bringing happiness to me.

REFLECTIONS

Reflections on the water, a wind stirring the trees,
Whispering secrets to tall green reeds.
A castle, its symmetry broken by the breeze,
Wavers and is lost in stagnant weeds.
Foreboding smote, leaping my heart,
Fleeting thoughts, omissions and circumspect deeds.
Crowded now, relating a part to this desolate place
That rooted me here, with its changing face.
Reflections flooding, streaming fluid from the brain,
Shimmering pictures leaping from near years and afar,
Dancing out to the horizon, to a rising star.

Reflections undulating in the strange eerie light,
Settle somewhat, the wind now gentle, abating, just right.
Nature allowing a momentary lull
Of turbulent emotions, of which my heart did mull.
Showing a steel grey mirror for eyes, piercing the night,
A flame to quench, memories to still.
Tormenting dreams, exalting thought,
All my yesteryears creeping at will.

A willow seemed to weep, her fronds reflecting woe,
Trailing bedraggled in the lake's constant flow.
I felt chilled with its wash, as if turned to stone,
Melancholy breeding, inadequacy to tone.
Rustling trees in silhouette related so,
Now tipped with silver in the moon's late show.

Reflections now shimmered in a different light,
Staying my mind's wallowing plight
The scene was the same, but there was beauty around,
As the lake now silvered, complemented the ground.

Reflections reflected, the picture was mine,
The significance reflected, I knew I was free this moment in time,
The aura had brightened, I was once again me.
What had swept my hallucinating fancies away,
Brought a miraculous calm, in a nightmare's sway.

Had my soul responded to my mumbled prayer,
As reflections had stirred, had caught me there?
I walked from the water, the moon showing the way
To reflect on reflection, and the dawning new day.

REMEMBERING

I sit by the fire watching it die,
The room so full of the past, it brings a tear to my eye.
I wanted to relate, willed someone there,
The moment nostalgic, needing someone to share.
I wanted the family, who had made it their own,
Who had filled it with dreams, that had seeded and grown
In young men, with a faraway look in their eyes,
Mulling over ambitions, cocooned in the brain,
Unfulfilled they burst, melting away like snow in the rain.
War burrowed deep, took the joy from this room,
Left a broken heart, to weep in the gloom.
Prone to reminiscing, to stifling tears,
Left with only memories of the wasted years.
The fire flickered, I acquiesced its demise,
The shadows beckoning, distorting strong
Halucinating faces, that once did belong,
Had a right to a life planned in this room,
A life of fulfilment, with love that did loom.
But with no culmination.
"Proceed," was the order to a soldier's kit
And tomorrow became a zero,
Where body and soul did not fit.
I cry out now at the memory, holding the past,
Foolishly wanting it so much to last.
As I sit by the fire, the moment sapping my will,
So please God, let light, let reason, in my heart instil
Vision for a new life, in this room so still,
Blessed peace for acquiescing, coating the pill.

REMINISCE

Let us tell it in rhyme, not in words of mime,
Repeating, repeating just the right line.
Visualise a vista, beyond the beat of the rain,
As you look through the window and cudgel your brain.
You can sail along on a pine-skirted loch,
Climb heavenly peaks, reaching the top.
A stroll in the moonlight can do incredible things,
And nostalgia is mixed with the immediate it brings.
Beautiful memories out of the past,
Twining dreams and reality, that don't fade, for they last
Forever in a circle, going round in your brain,
Folding to emerge with a certain refrain.
Precision has crept from somewhere out of the dark,
Retrospect in time, showing the part,
The dim glow of the jigsaw you could have solved years ago,
With the pieces you held, but did not as yet know.
You think of the water, its smooth silver sheen,
Emotions rising, in the heightened gleam,
Surrounded by places and people, who lost out on the day,
But as always in life, it just turned out that way.
The jigsaw was broken,
Kept just as a token,
A human repeat, this dalliance with time
Remembered in moonlight from a flash in the brain,
A human repeat, allowed in the rain,
This recall so sweet, this reminisce of mine,
This rhyme.

RENEWAL

A crocus broke the winter's ground,
Fragmented with snow, and scattered around,
The seasonal cloak, but allowing its dew
To sparkle in spheres diverse, giving a view
To footsteps deliberating a potential thaw,
To staying vertical, or bruised from head to toe.

A silver moon had long since gone,
And out of Morpheus's arms once more the world's anon.
An owl goes to sleep, topsy-turvy maybe,
Nocturnal renewal the essence of life for me.

A winter sun brings surprise in a grey patch of sky,
Makes a heart renewed, without asking why?
No words, just thoughts, teasing the brain,
The present, the future, singing a happy refrain.

I have weathered my walk, as many winter's say,
The crocus braving the elements, a symbol of nature's way.
Apprehension quite human, life's search a display,
A renewal of dreams, for a beautiful day.

RETROSPECT

Goodbye to summer, your long days are gone,
Your sun grows cold, with the moon taking on
The benevolent role of prompting night from day,
Its wash of silver a lure, to dream away.

Autumn leaves mingle rosy and gold,
Before winter's dance blustering cold.
Forsaken woodlands sway and weave,
Acquiescing the bounty the wind drifts and heaves.

Serrated mountains in air like wine,
Boast a wooded cloak in dark verdant pine.
Impervious majesty, secretive and stark,
Immune to the tree stripped bare to its bark.

Awaiting winter's enhance, its wrappings fine,
Of a sparkling frost, the encouraging sign
That snowy drapes are on their way,
Giving a naked tree a softer line
To withstand the holly's prolific spray,
Its red berries in cycle, in glorious array.

A wonderland of nature, the arbiter of the day,
Still sedating summer, and appeasing spring
In perpetual motion, the inevitable rota the elements bring.
Being human I sigh, I cry for the moon,
For an Indian summer, whilst yearning for June.
I need the warmth, the glow of an orange sun,
Pondering the seasons lost or won.

ROSIE'S DAD

"Rosie, Rosie," I was at the door of number six,
Calling my best friend, where I was free to mix
With all who went through that ever open door,
That grated and stuck as you pushed, on the bare stone floor.

In this house I was happy, felt really me,
Everyone was treated as equal you see.
It was the same at Maggie's, down the middle of the street,
If only ours was like these, full of friends you could meet.

But my mother was a widow, and always out,
Always the one to get talked about.
Rosie let me in, beckoning with her eyes,
And I looked round the house, that could not disguise,
The poverty, the wearing, the making do,
Maybe more so than most,
But taken for granted, for it was all that we knew.

It was Saturday noon, just the right time of day,
To be in the swing, and go along with the way
Things were conducted at number six,
Where all the news and scandal, dropped about like hot bricks.

Rosie's dad gave me a smile,
Looking up from t' Midday, he'd been studying some while.
For a paper and pencil graced the boiler top,
Where he sat with one hand, round the handle of a rather large pot.
Taking a last sup he held it out to me,
"Mek a fresh brew lass, it's cold this tea."

I rinsed out the pot, at the stone slop-stone,
Then waited for t' kettle, which was rather prone
To take a long time, to come to the boil,
On t' coal fire range, blackened and furred where t' smoke did coil.

Door was opening again, and I cringed at that door,
With its grating and rasping a scraping the floor.
It was Wilf, one o' t' regulars, paper in hand,
Fingering down t' page, saying when he found,
"It came in second again, but I'll back it today,
For it had made t' running all o' t' way."
"Aye," was all Rosie's dad did say,
Sitting patiently by t' fire awaiting his tay.
Then two o' t' kids came in shouting,
"Will there be any dinner today?"

But one of them, Freddie, spied a burner onta floor.
That quietened him, he was off, through t' middle door
Where Jimmie t' lodger wi' t' gospel in his hand,
Sat on a chair knowing lay o' t' land.

"Now none o' that smoking, thy art only a kid,"
But Freddie just grinned and lit up his squid.
Soon room filled wi' neighbours, all benevolent of face,
Each boasting their horse would win in a race.

For Rosie's dad was a runner, and now refurbished with tay,
Turned his attention once more to me.
"Now come on lass, get your skates on, and wi' our Rosie do a glide,
O'er road ta Jack Waterworth's, for t' time won't bide."
And glide we did, for we were two o' the three
Saturday runners ta t' bookies, an' kept at it, aye well past tea
Time, for as I recollect, sun always did shine,
And in between running, we spent our own time.

151

Happy as children, sometimes washing our hair,
And combing it out to dry in the sunshine there,
Sat on a donkey-stoned step, leading out o' t' backyard,
Pleasantly warm, not caring how hard.

Rosie would put rags in, twining strands of hair around each one,
But ten to one,
When nearly finished we'd get a call from Rosie's dad John,
Which had us flying like the wind again, a late bet to put on.

Poor as Lazarus, with hardly a rag to our back,
A sanding t' bare floor, when mopped and dry,
Or laying newspapers or sacking for t' feet,
For at least to walk by.

And Rosie's at Sunday was something ta see,
Four kids stood in a bowl in the slop-stone,
Each one in turn washed down by me.
Same bowl wiped up table, then went round t' floor,
With its donkey-stone stripe,
Its white usual decor.

Then came the moment, all the chairs round t' table were placed,
For John and his Mrs. had no time to waste,
To start playing whist, wi' friends that went on and on,
Wi' Rosie and me, taking count who lost and who won.
If Rosie's dad won, to Emma's shop we did run,
For tea and sugar in penny packets, and for afters a yesterday's bun.
We bought a quarter of corned beef, which for meat was in lieu,
A pan of potato hash was stirred, with an onion too!

And if an Oxo was handy that went in the stew
That was eaten with bread, and it made for a really good day
With of course a good brew,
Did someone mention tay?
Of course that went without say!

Aye tea was the mainstay,
It warmed t' cockles of your heart,
And it was surely Rosie's dad's stand by,
And the brew a ritual apart.

SCANDAL

Tongues like silk, dicing with words,
Bodies girating in moving herds.
Stance and arms, accentuating a specific theme,
A flaunting knowledge of what had been.

Performers drunk, filling the ears of the throng,
Tuned to the moment, erstwhile drawn out too long.
Quenching the thirst of bored souls,
Adding colour with innuendo to a sleazy goal.

Relishing the fall of some unfortunate, who
Had fallen by the wayside, with the 'I told you so's' spouting on cue,
The world outside their door, having disappeared in the air,
With no spiral to run through, to glean, or grab a share.
To succour from the flotsam, a tangible care.

To relate the heartache, from scandal tossed manifold about,
Sucked dry by leeches, avid gossips, that flout
Charity, trust, being harbingers of lies, yes tongues like silk,
With a viper's ink.

Tumbling words that push the heart
Into a pit of inadequacy, a hopeless despair,
Needing someone to share
A deep understanding, of a living nightmare.
Did you happen to obtrude, be one of them there?

SELF

There is only one world, it revolves around me,
And I bet this rates favourably with the view that you see.
Never thinking of others, what you could do, or might,
Methodically pushing, such thoughts out of sight.
And to cries of anguish, our ears are deaf in the night.

Routine tasks, a must you say,
Well maybe some, but not all each day.
Social schemes in our brain, obscure all else around,
Puffed up with importance they claim all of the ground
Where worthwhile things struggle to grow,
The view so narrow, we pass not caring to know.

Always busy elsewhere, we are ready to shelve,
The whys and wherefores, in which we don't delve.
Reasons are lulled, abstinence is right,
We just go around with what **we** need in sight.

Filling our lives with personal zeal,
Allowing an odd throw of sympathy for those who feel
The crack of the whip, and the hunger bell,
That gripes their innards, like a gnawing knell.

Our eyes are open, but see no light,
And our ears remain deaf to the cries of the night.
There is only **me**, and the immediate around,
Don't we deserve our pleasures, having worked and found?

Yes, but others have plodded, and somehow lost
The struggle and fight, and now count the cost.
We don't think we are unkind in what we do,
But how do we treat the unfortunates who

Live daily in shadows, painted smiles on their face,
Who yearn for the sun, to be back in the race,
To come in from the cold, and gain in the thaw,
A spot of happiness, a place their own to know.

Let us remember their needs, their possessions so few,
Let us remember they have feelings, like me and you.
Inadequate as they are, let us hold out a hand taking them on a par
With understanding, and kindness, without any bar.
Let us see with their eyes,
Give comfort and love, and help them to rise.

SEVEN BROWN SPARROWS

Seven brown sparrows swung on my washing line,
Winging into my tree, before darting back to climb.
Light as thistledown, streaking to and fro,
A bit of preening ahead, swivelling around,
Waiting for crumbs to drop onto the ground.

It was raining again, a brown flash dive bombs the tree's heart,
Chirping, and shaking the leaves apart.
Irate neighbours, a few years ago, cut down my tree,
Complaining the leaves scattered into their yard
When October deemed to blow too hard.

For over a year I felt bereft,
Gazing sadly at the stump, all I had left
Of my tree, near the wall in the corner, strangely drab and grey,
A kin to myself, with only a backyard to view all day.
No greenery swaying, over cement and stone,
No little brown sparrows, perched and prone
To swing to and fro on my washing line,
Making brief contemplation of my tree, a time happy, benign.

The winter passed slowly, incessant rain, ice and snow,
And the wind, O that wind, how it did blow.
But I had lost my weather vane, my vibrant tree,
Bending with each gust, quite visible to see.

My tree was many things, besides pleasure to me,
Blossoming in May with budding greenery, giving its perfume free.
It was the turn of the year, surprisingly mild,
As sweeping the yard where debris had piled.

I spotted a thin pale, weaving trail on the bark of the stump,
A sprouting of green, opting to live, to spite the neighbours,
And helped by the rain.
All year long it steadily grew,
With a handful of sparrows hovering over to view.

Now everything is as it was before
My tree has life, giving my yard its natural decor.
Determined to grow
Just as before.
Inviting seven brown sparrows onto my washing line,
Chirping and swinging into its heart,
To lend moments of happiness for me to take part.

SHADES OF NIGHT

O dusky night, your enveloping shroud,
Nature's mystery and solitude, with fascination endowed.
Deep in the forest on the open plain,
In alleyways and doorways, your significance is the same,
Exudes an aura, the touch-line for fate,
With Mankind the element, a component of hate.
The welding of passions re-surge to your call
Of stars and moonlight, to enhance your role.
Imagination your ally, the usurper of calm,
The dreamer abetting on Morpheus's arm.
The moment, the past, the memory's warm.
O deep purple night full of silent sound,
Full of human endeavour to mysteries around.
Forever a sop in the Universe,
Forever eternal, commanding all reimburse.

SIR GALAHAD'S HEROES

Calculated destruction, man destroying man,
A scarring holocaust,
Fire and flames in the wind's roar a merciless fan.
Traumatic tragedy zoomed down from a plain
With spleen to injure, to kill, to maim.
Brave heroics, agony, war spews her disdain,
Freezing elements abetting, helping them in vain.
But danger, no deterrent to the will to do,
To human emotions from a steadfast crew.
Winched with fortitude from cloying smoke,
From burning oil, the bomb did invoke
Comrade trapped in a burning tomb, beneath a smouldering hull
Destiny, Nemesis, call it what you will,
Life's swept away in the urge to kill,
An aggressor's bidding, reaping its fill.
A black silent tug, men in vigil ready to do,
Stifled tears finding release in the remaining few.

Solemnly a bugle blares the *Last Post's* sad refrain,
And *Land of My Father's*, the hymn it sings and rings.
Human sadness and emotions, from lads stood there,
Tumultuous hearts vulnerable, evident inadequacy hard to bear.
Bluff Cove was the place, Bluff Cove will be the name,
Remembered forever in time,
Where no one did see braver lads, as yours and mine.
Were giving their all, fighting for freedom fine.
The Welsh Guards, First Battalion were struck down by a fluke
In the cause of liberty, by advantage took.
Sir Galahad's last moments with a turn of fate,
Hell's sinking into a deep, deep sleep.
Cradling its heroes in glory, in eternal remembrance,
Heaven's portals wide open. God bless them and keep.

SPANISH HAPPINESS

Dear Mr. Michael Portillo,

Memories are born with happiness, my memories of you will always be so. I knew your name and nothing more. I'd glimpsed you face in past demeanours, of whatever the current news attached to you.

On January 12th 1999, life was as it had been for years, too boring to say. The phone rang. It was my daughter Dorothy.

"Watch TV tonight mum, there is something to interest you on. It's a documentary called, *Great Railway Journeys*."

"Yes love. I have noted it. In fact I was just about to tell you to do the same," I replied.

She laughed, "I thought it would catch your attention, being about Spain."

And it did, I would not have missed it for the world, and my daughter knew it too.

I willed myself back into the past, my arthritic bones were forgotten, my limbs felt free and unfettered, as I remembered walking the cobble-stoned alleyways, where geraniums pots trailed their blossoms over balconies and walls, before emerging in the sunlight that was warm on my face. I recall with such happiness in my heart my first sight of mimosa growing wild. You see we took winter holidays; my husband had managed to overcome my fear of flying.

When I was a child, crenelle castles I saw on occasions on the newsreels of the penny pictures on Saturday afternoons, which brought to me such dreams of Spain. It seemed to be such a romantic place to be in, and it was enhanced with a song that was sung in all the appropriate moments, when the words were bounced along by a white ball moving across the screen, while a lady played the music on an organ from a box at the side.

It sort of dulled the horror we felt at the next caption thrown up on the screen of rows of Jack Boots marching. Trance-like bodies, carried rapier styled guns, as helmets glinted in the sun.

In a little Spanish town, 'twas on a night like this, went the song. Every time that I heard it sung I was in another world, a sort of will-o-the-wisp world of somewhere I could not comprehend; it was somewhere in my dreams. And all down the years when all you have are dreams, all things Spanish have stirred my emotions, and still do. So each holiday we took, for a little while at least I was where I always wanted to be - *In a little Spanish* Town.

Past snatches of memory told as you journeyed along were easing the yearnings of my heart, and were bringing back the happiness. I write poems and have sent you my Spanish ones, I suppose they will be destroyed when I die, like the Fairy Stories I have written that sit here on my pouffe waiting to be discovered.

Thanks Mr Michael Portillo for your *'Great Railway Journeys'*, you made my day, and gave me a little hope. If only I could see Spain again, if only I was free. Arthritis go away!

Adios Amigos

STEPHEN

A teenage boy, straight and tall smiled as we stepped on the shore.
The Statue of Liberty also proclaimed, superior, supreme to the fore.
Vigilance her waiting game, her torch held high, her green aged robes,
and crown, symbols of Majestic fame.

Cousins meet cousins, you shake a quartet of hands, your family
and you taken as you are. Greetings, kisses and chatter, relaxing
where you stand, with smiles all round. Stephen the boy leads the way
to the car.

You are driving now through warrens of stone that tower excitedly
and blot out the sky, dwarfing throngs of people hurrying by. They are
immune to the beatings of your heart, and unaware of the wonder of
which you are now a part, of this exuding humanity in the treadmill of
life. Their purpose, intent, is a secret locked within strife.

The spectacular, the strange, spilled from sidewalks, from taxis
with screeching brakes and rearranged in the gauge of hustle that
makes its assault on your ears in this mad, mad whirl.

This was a cue for Stephen to allay our fears. Our attention is
caught as he goes into his commentary of New York. Places of legend
leap before our eyes, palpitating our hearts, bringing such happy
sighs. Too full for words we let the city roll by with Stephen's how's,
when's, and why's, just one big flow of explanations that you grip
now that he takes it more slow. And a red light gives us time for a
quick look around, to savour famous names, and the pleasures we
have found. And here it all happens when the night lights show. Neon
and blinking in a riotous blaze of colour, showing adverts that we
know.

Our elation grows, like the pride in Stephen's eye, as he points out
Broadway that we are now driving by. Demo's the underground.
Rockafella Centre, and so. It is now The Empire State Building, from
the highest to the low, for restricted is the view from the car where we
are, going under now yards of criss-cross steel rearing in rust, and

making your head rear, as it seems to cry out for a lick of paint, with all the overhead transport adding queasy, to faint.

All is mixed with the hustle and raring to go. You wonder if there is anywhere nice and slow? But it has all come true, it is no longer just a dream. We really are here in New York, and I feel like a Queen. With Stephen's information between the stops and the goes. Exuberant eloquence that just flows and flows.

Then suddenly there is space, the concrete is slipping away, we are cruising now, leaving objects man-made for a quieter spot near a verdant glade. It seems all the more sweet for what we've left behind. We see swaying trees and green shades of all kinds. This is where hills are free to roll, swathed in this green, where the air is breathable, fresh and clean, where flowers can grow, pleasing the eye, where the horizon is free to meet the sky.

We approach Stephen's Kingdom, and notice that his pleasure has grown for all the world over, there is no place like home. Fluid now, he reaches his norm, his phrases falling on the country air, for it is delightful America with a certain flair. And don't we detect the maternal Scottish brogue, as he answers our questions with never a goad? Full of surprises he has baked us a cake, with **'Welcome Cousins'** piped on its wake.

Wherever we wish he propels us along, ready to help if we put a foot wrong. We wished to visit a church; there was no problem there, we wanted to visit a store; all our requirement he would bear. For all things to Stephen are to be enjoyed, *savoir faire*. For he is on the ball, his probing knows no bounds, into people, into life, so we have found. A bundle of energy, he goes on with schedules that he has planned, literally talking us into the ground. And now we just nod to acknowledge the sound.

But everyone thanks God for Stephen, and his talkative ways, for there is no one quite like him for brightening dull days. He is part of our family, bonded in love, giving thanks for small mercies to Him up above. Jolly and happy, and taking so much care, with a wonderful welcome provided for us cousins from over there. And maybe someday Stephen will have talked his way into a spiral of wealth, not forgetting the happiness and health.

But wait, what is missing, my brain's in a whirl. Why just what comes naturally, of course, it's a girl!

SUMMERTIME

A caterpillar eats another leaf,
A cricket chirps in loud relief,
Timing the bee with its buzzing drone,
The forest is alive, and always prone
To credit all creatures with the right of way,
Nature's rhythm through night and day.
Procreating their world in a flurry of wings,
In feathery down, tiny beaks open, eyes seeking around.
Wild flowers in meadows a mix in summertime,
Blow in the wind barley stalks in rhyme.
A bee and a poppy condoning the code,
A jackdaw cawing its own special mode
Of summer madness, the cycle won't wait.
Trees, swaying leaves, emphasising the date.
Dappling coins of gold on shady tracks and hedgerows fold
Over a babbling brook, meandering at will,
Lending its surge to an old water-mill.
The summer sun adding sparkle, its droplets clean,
Dancing into a frothy ocean.
A wild rose, its face tinged red,
Its prickly leaves trailing water's rough stony bed.
O maturing summer with a nebulous flow,
Run true to form, and don't let go.
Of you poignant aura, your meadows of hay,
Your mellowing of emotions at the end of the day.

SWEET RECALL

I gazed at the house across the way,
Idly doing nothing; it was the close of day.
Noticing the sun sparkling the windowpanes,
As shadows moved slowly on the wane.
A shutter opened in my brain,
Letting me peep into yesterday,
So long ago, so far away.
Memories danced of another day,
No cares or worries, just sun-filled days
That were filled with play.
There was Rosie, Nora and Florence too,
And Maggie lived at number 42.
Our street was so long, with windows bright,
And round about six, practically every night,
Neighbours would squat on their donkey-stoned steps,
Talking, arguing, about money and debts.
Never budging an inch, their view always right,
Not forgetting to fawn on the horse backers who had won bets,
For a soft touch they would make on the following day.
Then changing the theme,
A scandal would unravel nice and slow,
When it came to the spicy bits,
The listeners would crack on that they didn't know.

Now the end of our street looked onto Cairo Mill,
Which slanted down the side of a hill.
While the other side boasted a mill, much bigger still,
Hence it got its name, it was called Shed Hill.
Which was appropriate being flanked don't you think
With mills the same?
When darkness fell the hill was our delight,
And checking no Bobby walked in sight,

We ran swiftly to where a gas-lamp loomed,
Its iron splendour blinking in the night,
Caught us children looping our ropes over its arm,
Swinging, swinging round its base,
Where we set off with our foot to heighten the race
On Shed Hill at a furious pace.
Further down was Peter Pig's Farm,
But strictly in daytime,
When the sun was warm,
We would, that is if we could, sneak out together,
Go off to play, meandering down a sandy track,
With laughter and talk, doing this and that.
To cross a meadow, where a lazy stream,
Ran over moss and stones,
Some black, some cream.
We would invent a castle sat under a tree,
And fight off a dragon, that role was always for me.
Then Rosie would scream,
"Let's rescue the Queen."
And having our shoes off we would splash through the stream.
Very soon we would tire, we'd have enough of that,
So off again we'd hurry back
To where the meadow joined the track.
To go blithely on treading where we could,
On the largest stones to avoid the mud.
Climbing deftly over a well-worn stile,
We had reached our goal.
Hence I recall,
The chatter, and especially the smile
That I gave to Nora, who always said,
"I could walk forever, well maybe a mile,
On these soft-trodden leaves near ferns that grow,
In different shades, wherever you go.
Come on, let us go deep under the trees,
Where the tallest bluebells grow."

Nothing loath, we did just that,
And in the lush verdant aura away from the track,
We filled our arms with luscious bluebells,
Moving trance-like amid their pungent smells.
Later, aware of our acquired bouquets,
We'd realise that it was nearly the end of the day,
And slowly homeward, we would wend our way.

It seems funny now after years have slipped away
That I can still remember things as clear as day.
Through sun and shadows on a backyard wall,
Flashing a memory of sweet recall,
The time and the place, and even the day
You spent with friends along the way,
When we were young, happy days of play,
Sweet recall, now so far away.

TELL ME PLEASE

Well what can I say,
What would you really like me to say?
How should I begin to express my view,
String words to vie with your special way.
What topic is the darling of your heart?
If only I knew, I would make it more a part.

What would you really like to see written down,
An elusive query, bringing forth a frown?
Is it the affluent world that could bring the smallest sound
Of a subconscious murmur of delight,
Or the sophistication, their values and ethics in constant flight,
More yours to beat to the tune of the elite.
Or the world of nature, where survival's a must,
With nocturnal calculations agog in the night.

If it's none of these things, well what should I try?
Is it the dew on a rose, or a seagull's cry,
The last one home, streaking the sky,
Where a glorious sunset, colouring a tranquil sea,
Could touch anyone's heart, pray what could it be?

Is it the moon at night, with its passive roll
Lighting your way under a purple sky,
Probing, nurturing its mysteries with stars twinkling by.
Or is it just wit, effervescent and free,
Or a highbrow thesis; well whatever it may be
It just passes me by, I am just mundane and plain,
Full of questions, without answers, that tease my brain,

Waiting the right moment to let them unwind,
Eloquent and startling, so rewarding I would find.
Appeasing curiosity, the ever wondering too,
What turns you on to your point of view.
Are the basics the same, and what and who, is the real you!

TERRACED HOUSES

Terraced houses, with backyards too,
Very ordinary, without a view.
Where trees peep over some of the walls,
And flowers are grown in quite a few.
Rows of houses painted well,
Swept and scoured, as you can tell
When you run your eyes over steps and yards,
That are washed and stoned with 'Bradford Hards'.
Neat little windows set in colour-washed walls,
Pleasing to the eye, the way the curtain falls.
Draped round pots, in ceramic and brass,
Holding plants, or whatever the owner wants.
Corner shops busy, with people around,
Their jingling bells adding to the sound
Of screeching car brakes that stop to vie
With each other, for a park nearby.
For it's the mid-week football match tonight,
Played at Turf Moor across the main road in sight.
Children screaming at their usual games swell the din,
Getting tempers inflamed of irate fans taking the shortest way
To the game, they have thought of for most of the day.
While barking dogs, who should not have been there,
Dash over roads, running everywhere.

A familiar scene in this part of town,
Did I see you look bored, did I see you frown?
Well pity us mortals whose lot it is
To live among it, be it a her, or a his,
Amongst the streets with uniform doors,
Whose routine life is to survive, and scrub floors.
But who sometimes sigh for a way out of the rut,
The lucky few do find one, others haven't the gut.

Just delving in dreams, where visions flow,
As far remote as summer snow.
Like a win on the pools, with a chance to attain,
The where with all, to a turn in the lane
Of terraced houses and backyards too,
That bog you down and swamp your view
Of the outside world, set in fields afar, where trees can grow
Without a wall,
And flowers can bloom, with no restrictions at all.
Where per chance to dream,
Just as you are, you walk through colours and shades of green
Right out to a cadillac car,
You float along on a dream a day,
To a castle, all mellowed and gold,
For you are a Princess, having found you Prince,
And you know you will never grow old.
Don't laugh at these musings, with a superior smirk
For in each of these houses at some time do they lurk.
But now I am back
On the down to earth track
Resigned to houses sometimes maligned.
Back to the knowledge behind the exteriors there,
The heartaches and struggles sometimes too hard to bear.
As the women polish and sweep, then swill the yard,
Finishing off steps with a 'Bradford Hard'.
It's all in the game,
Has always been the same.
You carry on, with dreams giving a helpful perk,
Through the daily grind, getting rid of the dirt.

With an occasional burst of temper as well
You take it out on the children, you shout and you yell,
Knowing in the houses next door
Your voice will sound like a bell,
But you couldn't care less for by the noise down the street,
Someone else is at it and fighting pell-mell.
Just a little weary now, but you have learnt to be hard,
You slam and bolt the door leading to the yard,
To shut out the din, and language some,
Can call quicker that reading a Bingo card.
Feeling far from adequate you tend to be sad,
You think of the good, but it's mostly the bad,
Wishing passionately for a house with more than a yard,
You think, but you know you will have to stop or go mad,
For aren't there thousands who have not, and wish that they had,
For them a house on a terrace, without even a yard,
Would never rate bad,
And to think of it as heaven would not be very hard.

THE BOOK

It was a bleak January morning, and not very encouraging as the heavily-ladened grey skies threatened any minute to open heaven's hard. But not to be deterred, I wrapped myself up ready for the weather, and stepped outside into an icy wind, that blew full in my face, whipping strands of hair around my fur hat, whilst I constantly strove to push it back out of my eyes.

I was making my way down to town with a glow of anticipation filling my heart, taking me in flights of fancy that were as strong as the blustering winds that I was struggling against to reach my goal.

At last I was climbing the last of a dozen steps to push my way through the somewhat stiff doors of the public library. I had made it, and rather out of breath I paused, as my eyes took in the layout of the highly polished hallway. I was assailed with the longing to bury my nose into the bronze and yellow ferny display, and bending to do so, their pungent aroma satisfied my sense of a Christmassy smell, that was so nostalgic to me.

Feeling better now I let the moment go, observing the half glass panels of two doors just across the hall, that were strategically placed, one each side of a stretch of panelling and glass with the words 'IN' and 'OUT' picked out in gold lettering on each door.

Could my objective lie within these doors? Somehow I thought not. My quest was for a book on Literary Agents, which I could borrow from the library, but where was such a classification housed?

Further along the shiny passage I spotted a glass plate suspended on chains, and now wafting slightly from the draught from a door above a double flight of stairs, banged in exuberance by an eager young man, who flashed down to my level, with papers flourishing in his hands. The glass plate read, 'REFERENCE LIBRARY', with a red arrow pointing up the stairs.

I hurried on up, crossed the small landing, and walked through the swing-doors into a long oblong room, with tables, chairs, manuscripts, maps, books and people, all totally immune to my intrusion of their individual digestion of importance. I made for the desk, where a young lady greeted me with enquiring eyes, momentarily letting go of her morning task. It ran through my mind that everything was just right. I had gained attention without a tedious wait, and from the friendliest face that I have ever encountered behind a public desk.

Realising swiftly that I did not know exactly what to ask for, I made a few rather disjointed phrases, in the asking of who to write to, in order to get some stories published?

The young lady was a genius, as she understood me immediately, and she tapped the book she had been thumbing through before my interruption. Smiling sweetly she said, "I must have known you were coming today, for this is just the book you want. It is the current Writer's and Artist's Year Book." She flicked through a few pages asking what category I wanted?

My reply of, "Children's Stories," had her reading snatches here and there.

Announcing, "Sorry I've really spent enough time on your enquiry," she said, "I will just go and see if the previous years are available as this one cannot be taken out."

I watched her walk the length of the room before disappearing through a door at the end. Apprehensively I waited, was I going to be lucky, or would all my excited anticipation of borrowing the book come to nothing, leaving me still without the knowledge which I sought?

The Librarian was returning now, had she found it? Yes, she carried a book in her hand.

I let out a sigh, then gave her a smile.

She was behind the counter now, and she produced a slip of paper. She then asked me for my name and address for the reference book, which she then placed into the said book, then stamped the date on *my* book, as I was now calling it.

Pleasantly she said, "You will find what you are looking for presumably on page 355."

I thanked her, popped the book into my bag, and left the library. As I battled my way home against a blustery east wind, I became wrapped in a rosy glow of elation, for I had got the book, and not even those first dampening drops of winter rain, which soon quickened into an outright deluge that lashed down on me, could quell the well being in my mind.

Soon I was home, and could not get out of my hat and coat fast enough. I hung my outdoor clothing up to dry, and hastily unzipped my boots, removed them, then thrust my feet into my slippers ready to flop into my fireside chair.

With the book in my hand I eagerly turned to page 355. This would surely prove that the excitement that I felt in my heart was justified, I thought. I read the preliminary information, general advice and all that I had never even given a thought to.

Quickly reading further, I hastily skimmed over warnings and suggestions, taking them in as a matter of form that surely could not relate to me. Half-way down the page now, I was getting the gist of what was expected of a would-be writer, and found the potential was staggering.

Suddenly I felt deflated, and all my exhilaration ebbed away. Hastily I ran through the listed agencies and their preferences, trying to ignore the more professional and technical bits.

Dancing before my eyes now, were films, theatre and broadcasting work. I felt rather lost and chilled, and crouched nearer to the fire for warmth, if only the material kind. Had I really dared to hope that any of these clever sounding creatures, in their smug efficient offices would deign to cast their eyes over **my** children's stories, fairy stories at that, and even written painstakingly in longhand, with intermittent badly defined letters, due to an arthritic hand?

I sighed again, saying to myself, "Well hopefully there is always tomorrow, and where there is life there is always hope."

I was just about to close the book when my eyes read the word, 'Children'. This had eluded me so far.

So speaking to myself once more I said, "One agency amongst the many, unless I go through the book. I will write to this one," and my mind seemed to be soaring again.

After finishing my meal and the ensuing evening chores that followed, I was still dreaming in front of my cosy fire, allowing the elements of a cold January day to creep up on me, for that is surely what life is all about.

THE FIRST CHRISTMAS NIGHT

It is not very far where you have to go,
Just follow the footprints in the snow
To a portico building, imposing no doubt,
But the footsteps don't stop there, just go round and about
To a lowly stable, opened under a star,
Three wise kings have followed with gifts from afar,
To kneel midst the animals, in adoration where
Mary and Joseph's new-born babe huddles there,
With angels hovering in silence, as the star shines bright,
Bringing Peace and Goodwill and Jesus, on that first Christmas night.

THE FIRST SNOW OF WINTER

The first snow of winter had fallen in the night; the sky was heavy with the promise of more to come. In bleak morning light I let my eyes stray over the soft white blanket stretching down my way.

The silence around was like a dirge. Dare I step out, but where was the verge? The long mill wall looked strangely grey, with its mould of snow smoothly rounded that way. The wind had piled it like a cocoon. It matched mill windows swathed in drifts and skips of cotton, who all wore white shifts.

The hump-backed bridge was a picturesque sight, rating high marks for the worker by night, who had topped its hump, that tended to break with a glistening surface, making it look whole, in muffs of white with a curving roll.

Enhanced was a tree, white banded too, now drooping heavily underneath the load, and as I watched snow flopped onto the road. A bird flew down breaking the symmetry of the snow, pecking furiously all around, no doubt bewildered by the state of the ground.

I stepped out then, having donned high boots, elated at the silence and the crunch of each step, softly finding solid ground. Something stirred within my heart, but whatever it was I just let it go, walking on in rapture over the snow.

Always an early riser, I had caught my world, had waited for the dawn to savour its beauty, and walk all alone, before its cloak of white could be defiled, could slither away and melt and reveal the sight of mills and houses with their care-worn faces striving through time to age with grace, and compete with the world over the bridge with green vistas and trees stretching onto a ridge.

The first snow of winter had lightened my day, had touched my heart, and though some disparaged its fall, happiness had crept into the best day of all.

THE MAGIC DELL

The fairies gave a party, inviting all to come
Dancing along a border of white Chrysanthemum.
Fronds of drooping Spruce splayed out and swayed
Its leaves all a-whisper for the fun had just begun.
A green elf doffed his cap to a dwarf-like plant,
The wind's musical tones a rustling natural cant.
A starry eyed Daisy beckoned to the throng,
And a smiling Pansy told a Rose, the night was made for song.
For Dandelions, dew-ladened, a golden pollen dish,
To mingle with sweet Clover, a tit-bit not to miss.
A fairy danced a ballet, a light airy theme,
In and out of the Bluebells, dainty and serene.
A firefly brought his family, flashing high and low,
Showing mole and rabbit, the quickest way to go.
A small brown bird was singing, a grey squirrel joining in,
Stripy bees a buzzing, were adding to the din.
The Queen was now selecting the largest toadstool there
To place a cache of nuts, part of the tempting fare,
When a reedy croaking sound grew more strong,
Out puffed a green frog, who was trying out his song,
With animals, birds, and fairies doing really well,
Dancing in a frenzy beneath the magic spell.
The witching hour was chiming, the moon had cast a glow,
Shedding silver radiance upon the scene below.
The green elf's pirouette around a fairy ring,
Signalled time to all the party to disperse and sing,
"Hurry rabbit, scurry mole,
Magic spreads its final curtain call
Casting shadows, dispelling spells,
The arms of Morpheus embracing the magic dell,
To dreams once more for you to tell!"

THE PICTURE

The picture it hung in an old dark room,
In a backwash of yesteryears.
Dusty and ignored, and passed by in the gloom,
Streaked and coated with smears.
No one deigned it a fleeting glance,
Or looked for beauty in its demure stance.

Then suddenly startlingly out of the blue,
The quiet was stirred, and all around grew,
A tumult of voices and footsteps too!
Tramping on up from out of the hall,
To gaze at the picture on the wall.

Someone suggested the need for more light,
And reached for the switch, for a better sight.
Then excited voices rose and fell,
Debating half of the night.

Criticising, praising, some doubting as well,
With a voice raised in authority saying, "It was too soon to tell."
It was finally wrapped up and carted away,
To be dumped on a worn oak bench,
Where a tired old man, after being knocked up,
And finding it rather a wrench
Resignedly gathered the tools of his trade,
It was obvious, without any pride,
Thinking it was just another mundane thing,
For which he would eventually be paid.

He mixed the cleaners, and poured out some oil,
Taking care to lay out some foil.
Then the brushing, cleaning and scraping began,
Touching here, touching there, then more alert
He was suddenly aware
That the canvas he worked on,
Justified this urgency, and was something more than rare.
He let his skill override,
Pushing lethargy aside,
As he warmed towards his task,
Carrying on carefully, slowly dissolving the mask.

The mask that years of grime had built on,
The glow of a gown
In ruby silk, and on the tears in the eyes of the woman there,
Who was pleading, laying her soul bare,
For the life of her son,
The soldiers were taking at the point of a gun.

The light and shade were beautiful now, opalescent and all aglow,
The old man smiled, and wiped his hands, for now he did surely know
That no more would the picture be passed in the gloom,
Forgotten in some musty old room,
For with brush poised again,
He feathered it slowly round,
Revealing a much loved name.
Yes mother and son would bask in the light,
And hang in the hall of fame.

THE SILENT REAPER

Death, unexpected he stalks, nostrils a flare
No quarter allowed for the unwary there.
Arrogantly he takes human happiness away,
Adding sorrow to strife, immobilising all life.
The devil, his ally, as the Silent Reaper goes by,
Marking man's strife, another soul to claim, is the game,
In war, the ultimate sacrifice is his decree.
The flower of humanity along we go, you and me

THE TREE

The tree stood gaunt, near a hump-backed bridge, a sentinel for all to see. While across the way, a gabled house puffed smoke in coils of grey, slowly dispersing, silently slithering away.

The glowing windows of the house, bordered white with the snow that had fallen in the night, joined with the Evergreens in a superior smirk, at the tree bereft of leaves.

But the snow had excelled itself in its work, forming a special seal, with bands and muffs of white, and falling thickly, it had completed the deal, raising the tree to an elegant state, as its branches embraced the night.

The glow from the windows gilded the road. It was now a frozen beaten track, shining like a mirror over the bridge, and treacherous where wheels had furrowed a ridge, on journeys there and back.

Round a distant bend, and coming on strong, was the clip-clop of horses, with a coach pulled along. Throwing prisms of light from lanterns slung low, that changed the ghostly scene, lighting the hedgerows, till they hit the tree on its snow-clad arms, with a dazzling silver gleam, turning it swiftly into a living thing, like a quiver from a bow.

As a figure in red, trimmed with sparkling white, brought the coach carefully up to the right to hang a Holly wreath on a snowy-white branch. It was a lovely Christmas sight!

The gaunt old tree seemed to spruce up then, to stand more straight and tall, and regard the Evergreens across the way, with a smugness all of its own.

The coachman winked as he passed by, for he had more stops on the way, but the tree had rated the first of his gifts, for being on duty for Christmas Day.

It warned the traveller to slow on down at the hump-backed bridge to town, with its out-stretched arms it was a landmark, bright in its raiment of snowy-white.

THE WORLD

The rotating world slowly showing her face,
Colours rolling, etched in scrolls of lace,
Beneath gliding clouds puffed out with grace.
Crimson, gold, green, silver and blue,
Panoramas flaring, alternating anew.
From vivid to pale, with a quenching light,
As sombrely the blue changes to a shooting grey,
To a shroud tinged purple, ending the day.
Whatever the elements you wish to define,
On her axis stable, serene sublime.
She views the back-cloth of sun, moon and stars,
With resigned acceptance of love and wars.

Attracting probes from dimensions unknown,
Where is Apollo?
And on Olympus does Zeus still reign with a flair?
Or is Mars now his kingdom,
With his compatriots there?

Do out of space vagaries plot and steer,
From light years away, is Nemesis near?
The rotating world with its famine and strife,
Greed for power corrupting life.
But not calling its majesty, its night and day.
Its hurricanes, eruptions, sweeping destinies away.

The sun pays her licence, bestowing at will warming rays
On her chosen days,
Blazoning appreciation, on an appointed sphere,
Condescending to allow streaks to filter and smear,
The unfavoured pitch, the shadowy trail,
Where life is lived beneath a cloudy veil.

This world of ours, with its varied hues
With its fickle nature from the human views,
We take all subdued through the aeons of time,
Slipping each day through nightly folds.
Carrying us further away from familiar shapes, assuming many forms,
Conceiving giants, in man-sized garb,
Hatching destruction to harass and harm,
Defiling its beauty, commanding each living soul,
With venomous spleen, attaining their goal.

And yet, a low rising dawn turns from pearly grey,
Through a pinkish hue, to a golden day,
Gilding the roll of the downs, threading the old stone walls,
With a morning splendour, where crystal waters fall
From underground to flood and fill,
A natural hollow near a water-mill.
Where daffodils sway,
Neath a willow's splay,
Bowing profusely and stirred by the breeze,
Into a feathery trailing frieze.

A pleasant spot this one small niche
In the world so wide, with its poor and rich.
With wrestling emotions for hate, or love,
Let obeisance for the latter, come from above.
From some mystic heaven beyond a star,
Smoting the dominant in the time where we are.
To weave a spell, to delve in the fey,
With hope exuding along the way.
This world of ours with its beauty around,
Blending, manifest with the goodness we have found.

THEN AND NOW

There is snow on the hills over Pendle way,
But the sun is doing fine, to brighten the day.
I glimpsed filtering sunlight through a garden tree,
Filling my mind with summer, poppies in a meadow and a stripy bee.
A smattering of daisies star the grass
Around each newly-built, so recent, semi and flat,
Where terraced houses once stood,
Neighbours at the door, ready to chat.

But the wind is whispering, growing more strong,
To a black cloud obliterating the blue of the sky.
I was suddenly chilled, the immediate, darkly sat
Stopping flights of fancy, musings of the past and future,
And where to be at.

When the long days of summer would eventually arrive,
But alas not comparable with the ones I did survive.
Did they hold magic, those far away times,
When pleasures were simple, and the sun had its hat on,
As sung of in rhymes.

The snow over Pendle is so far away,
Like the youth I once had, setting foot on vistas bare,
And the Cathedral, yes once had made my day
Leading the heart of a child down a make-believe way
To revelations of happiness, a winter wonderland of joy,
Holly and Mistletoe at Christmas for each girl and boy.

When stockings filled with presents, an apple and orange
And chocolates boasted a bright new penny.
I knew friends that got these,
But I never got any!

Why's and wherefore's, too complicated to tell
The whole story.
Oh there were far too many
Ah well, don't look a me, ah well!

The wind still whispers as through all the changes there have been
And the garden tree's catkins, silver and greyey green
Know all the secrets spawned down the years,
And amidst all the elements of heartbreak and tears
The seasons emerge from winter, like hearts of people walking by
Then and now, sort of personal,
Something special, under your own piece of sky

THERE IS

A heaving garden under the sea,
A shelving secrets guarded fishily.
A beautiful mermaid, hair a flow,
A turtle her steed, his motion all set to go.
A fairy tale picture, a once upon a time
A delving of a destiny, buried in brine.
Translucent ripples, bubbling curtains of gold
Light shimmering the glitter, alternating green to an azure blue fold.
Shoals of fish in a trance-like glide,
Paying silent homage to a radiant bride.
Perpetual motion, the forever sea,
Colours that sway in flower-like corals,
Tentacles waving forming a kelp tree.
Oysters smiling, boasting a pearl,
For the pearl of the ocean, their golden girl.
A beautiful Princess, in silver and jade,
A sea-horse beckons, where Neptune's known to roam,
His snowy white charger magnificent, a tumbling foam.

Banishing the sea witch, with thunderous bells,
The sea's Kings, legion of legends safely hidden in vaults of shells.
Fathoms of mystery, under a fathomless sea.
Under a full moon's magic, exuding vision that be
Akin to the heaven's billion stars,
The roof, the floor, the fascinating lure, that never jars
From make-believe to reality,
Curiosity and dreams, such a beautiful world relating so,
In a fluid wonderland, that won't let go.

THERE IS SILENCE AROUND

There is silence around, let us keep it that way,
A small piece of heaven, a golden part of the day.
I have been through the rough, I have travelled around,
I have played with fire, to fall burned on the ground.
Misjudging the flame, the roaring sound.
Some ask if I care, the wheel still pulls me round.

The answer is somewhere, but to probe I don't dare.
Ignoring the innuendoes, with the insults I bear,
Let them all have their say.
What the hell, I don't care
There is silence around, let us keep it that way.

But the beat still goes on, the familiar refrain,
Taunting me, haunting me, round in my brain.
Shattering the silence, and casting the spell,
The spell of a witch screeching hell from hell.
Splitting the silence, like the toll of a bell,
The beat growing louder, forever the same,
Torturing my mind, taking hold of my brain,
Dragging me back with yesterday's knell,
With its damning dirge, its tolling bell.

Go away yesterday, O please go away,
There is silence around, let us keep it that way,
Should I revert to my usual days,
To the hectic nights and casual ways,
Painting the town with the rest of the few,
Revelling in the break, this parting from you.

Should I have a fresh theme, for my new scheme?
Who am I kidding as I dream,
In my private hell,
Hearing only the toll of a bell,
Sending me down with its intoned knell,
Its dirge, of hell to hell.

Go away yesterday, O please go away,
There is silence around, let us keep it that way!

THIS ENGLAND

This beautiful land, it holds my heart
With all my tomorrow's essentially a part.
Hope eternal is the magical key,
Nurturing secrets seeded in me.
Reality and freedom go hand in hand,
Aspiring thoughts swifter than sound.
Painting dreams that make a beautiful day,
Assessing nature, will-o-the-wisp and fey.
Valleys and mountains, a clear blue sky,
Full of solitude, in my happy pass by.
In the velvet night, conductive to sleep,
My brain rebels that date to keep.
Rising emotions fighting strong,
To assess time, the essence to belong.
This land gave me freedom, a niche in life,
To fashion at will, memories rife.
God in his heaven, created it so,
A hotchpotch for breathing destiny's flow.
A piece of the Universe, men fought to be free,
For England our heritage, for you and me.

THIS SPAIN

How many eyes have turned towards the sky,
Praying adversity to pass them by.
How many legions down the aeons of time,
Have hailed this land a challenge,
As a harbour from the relentless brine?
Conquering, acclaiming, with no option but to bide,
Their acquiescent destiny, the adhering toil.
Nurturing seeds of life on this foreign soil,
Warring loving, friend and foe
Evolving as one, this sun-kissed land, abetting so.
Children begot of new form and face,
No longer alien, this spreading race.
Mingling on the barren plain,
Relating suffering each the same.
Who were these people of what manner and abode,
To what aspirations their daily code?
Did they conceive with inbred grace,
With resigned fortitude for a super race?
And had they time to dream, not usual visions of night,
But the ponderous kind, fraught with solitude,
Of the first streaks of light?
Did they glean mysteries in a stark mountain range,
Fantasies exuding in its peak's misty roll
Of secrets locked in its cold grey stone.
A revelation to the hearts of a fugitive soul,
Crying out for light, for a receptive goal.
So rich in beauty, in shape, magnificent and strong,
A forever mark, a natural possession, proud to belong.
Immune to time, from age to age,
Watching life, the holocaust of man's outburst unleashed in rage.
Still stark and remote, with elements holding the key,
To the work of God, for all to see.

This patch of earth, kissed by the sun,
Its rivers, its fauna, its battlements scarred and holed,
Where man has excelled, laboriously turning an exquisite mould.
Intricate lines that curve and flow, transforming a wilderness,
With monuments fine,
Creating legends out of far away time.
Cathedrals, palaces, castles mellowed by night,
Breathing romance, neath the moon's pale light.
Pleasured all humanity, that has passed this way,
On baited breath, evolution giving us this day.

Alien craftsmen who found an alien soil,
Wove the basic pattern in a blended coil.
The imprint left on the heart and soul,
Instilling knowledge with pride, in their questing role.
And now their spirits sleep where they were slain,
No matter their ilk, how high, how low their blood
Was shed for peace to reign
And their bones lie cradled in this land, this Spain.
Mi Espanol queter vez y siempre.

THIS URGE

I have got this urge, this terrible urge,
It has got me holed, snookered and bowled.
It's a compulsive feeling that won't let go,
In my subconscious it lurks, ever ready to flow.
This yen for words within my brain,
The improvising and rhyming getting quite a strain.

I want to flee, yearn to get away,
Just to be normal, in an ordinary way.
The ironing waits, I don't cook anymore,
I have given into this thing, can't put a foot through the door.
All I do is look indifferently around,
Observing but not caring, just furtively searching.
Ah there they are, my addiction props,
And settling down only takes two hops.

To be at it again,
With paper and pen,
Arranging foolscap so,
With pen poised, capturing thoughts that form and flow.
I was told a hobby was relaxing, rewarding no doubt,
But by my own experience, this theory I flout.
For I am all to cock, going from bad to worse,
Putting sense into rhyme, for my current verse.
With the daily round loaded, weighing heavier
Than a millstone round my neck.
Nevertheless the craving I pursue, wanting to forget,
Scribbling my heart out, just writing by heck.

My room's somewhat different, though I am not really averse
To the disorderly array, which some would think a curse.
Instead of flowers in vases, biros are in,
Protruding in showers and splayed round the brim.
Littering piano and table, cornice and nook,
With all dimensions of paper, stuffed in any old book.
For when the fever is rife,
There ends the orderly strife,
With the nearest object at hand,
A vehicle of use, to command.

Familiar things come alive, take on new meanings and so,
I express them in writing, spelling out what I know.
Mostly the mundane pieces of life,
With awareness flaring into something fey,
To be specified in rhyme,
Embroidered words, lilting and gay,
Pouring out like a stream from an overworked brain,
Beauty seen in a sharper vein.

And that is how I while the hours away,
Cluttered but happy, writing in my illegible flow.
Words new to me, I did not know,
Surprise the element, my heartbeat taking along my rising ego.
Telling a story, improvised as sixty minutes
Turn to hours so quick do they go.

Where did it come from, this frantic urge
To write of situations exclusively in rhyme
Claiming priority, to all of my time?
Will it die a death, imagination spent,
Or surge in inspiration, with visions lent?

THREE ON A LINE

The purple skirt danced on the washing line,
Its tiers and flounces billowing fine.
Taking its rhythm from the wind,
Whose high spirits did nothing to rescind
The twirls in a jumper, blown high then low,
Its sleeves all a tangle in the welt below.

A blouse with its bobbles blowing free,
Puffed a swinging shape, saying, "Look at me.
How graceful I blow, my laces and bobbles straighten out as I go.
Surely it's your material and make up, that is prone,
To tangle and twist in a jumbled up cone?"

The purple skirt never answered, for she was quite unaware
Of the jumpers plight, just struggling there.
Then an extra strong wind, a mighty gust doing its bit,
Put the blouse in its place, a misshapen and questionable fit.
With bobbles and laces, a whirling body and arms in the sky,
It suddenly looked withered, with its neckline awry.

The purple skirt just smirked with her hem of lace,
Then spoke to the jumper with surprise on her face.
For the wind's intermittence had set it free,
Now who will be under the iron, the most of us three.

And billowing and swaying they chatted away
In the wind, who really had the last say.
Blowing the garments with gusts of frenzied power,
Into a swirling, swinging feminine bower.
And one thing for sure, they were all bone dry,
The purple skirt, the blouse and the jumper, a blowing in the sky.

TIME - LET IT BE

Time is the essence with a mythical book,
Inviting the Universe to ponder and look
At options, with emotions hurled into space,
In the hotchpotch life that we human's face.
A mother with a child creating destiny in time,
The outcome as mysterious as a mountain to climb.
Youth in its glory in its irrelevance to time,
Grasps the dross for the gold,
That waits in the night to be bought or sold.
The sequence hidden, found only in time,
O elusive mentor, chains cannot hold,
Impassive you roll all things to all men.
All revealing to whatever or when.
Acquiescence is sold,
Wasted years acknowledged a once upon a time,
So intimate we allow we are old,
O happy reminisce let it be
All life in all time is alleged as free.

TO SING, TO CRY

To sing, to cry, what rings the changes, what fuses the spark, stirring emotions in the brain's full range. From Orpheus's music on Olympus high, to Dante's inferno, crying to die. Visions roll with a song from your heart, the world is yours to take a part. To float on a cloud, see a rosy dawn bursting crimson, sensuous and warm.

Cascading waters exude with a song, glistening gem-like, gurgling away, to a clarity of tone, clear as a bell, a captured cadence as you walk through the dell. A meadowlark spears the sky, trilling a song as he soars on high.

Not to be outdone a gentle breeze sets up a murmur in a copse of trees, stirring the leaves to their own special song. Swaying in rhythm, claiming that they belong to this sun-kissed moment, this heavenly time, where mundane human's walk, with nature benign.

Sing with happiness that the Almighty has shown, where you can fill your heart from dusk to dawn. If your values are set in just the right key, if your eyes flash shrewd, take note and see. When a soul is weary, it needs a helping hand. When you give with love, all that you have, plotting a way through the desert, the cloying sand. Music is there for all to hear, to sing as you will, in your own special sphere.

Colours unfold, some part of each day, with the blend of light, before slipping away. You follow the rise and fall of a hill, with your heart in a tumult, you drink your fill of nature's beauty dotted around, pleasing ears are a tuned to its sound. A smattering of poppies, flamboyant and rare, seeded by the wind, to a cornfield there.

The dew on a rose, hiding its heart to prolong its fragrance, to linger longer, remain a part of this tranquil scene, set in verdant green. Where clumps of trees in a forever stance, picturesque in stature, sway and enhance an old world cottage over an old stone wall, where hollyhocks grow lush and tall, in an old world garden, sheltering all.

With a water-mill, now quiet and still, just a bird sanctuary on the side of the hill, overgrown with lichen, and out of date, resigned to the neglect, that has sealed its fate. All is watched and noted by an old

Willow tree, which the years have bowed and set free, to straggle at will, like a shimmering veil to the water's edge, in a leafy trail, a swishing frieze in rhythms in the freshening breeze.

Such things are a joy, but somehow you sigh. Some days you lose, will this be a day that you break down and cry? You probe your mind, wildly asking why? For nostalgia is creeping from out of the past, with emotions struggling to hold you fast. But the battle is on, to be set free, like the blossom that has burst pearly white on the tree.

You sing with joy as you walk away, feeling as light as thistledown, and under a spell, for something has stirred you out of your knell. Did a waft of revelation fill your jaundiced eye to the beauty of nature under God's sky, to this rolling Savannah of beautiful things? Can you hear music, and just know how your heart sings? Time let it be, whatever it brings.

TO TEMPER YOUR DAY

A zest for living, happiness brings
Faith through love, the staunchest hinge.
Welding humanity in reason for right,
A kind word, a smile, giving credence and light,
In a vulnerable world of suspicion and hate,
And a million obstacles, the self righteous bait.
Soul searching too long for what went wrong,
Give and take, the dimension of right and wrong.
Happiness creeping with hope on the way,
Faith can move mountains, love relative to all men,
Sought in a prayer, can work if we try for a beautiful day.

TOLERANT THOUGHTS

Tranquillity no man can mar,
The span of the ocean, the gleam of a star.
The deep purple void of rolling sky,
Mysterious infinity, exciting the eye.

Golden sands shifting, beneath spewing seas,
Perpetual motion, ever fluid, ever free.
Horizons beckoning a wanderer's dreams
Emotions stirring, and turbulent schemes.

It's happened, it's love, in the immediate where
Nature blossoms, in her craving to share.
Urges flow, feelings burst whole,
The world is there to grasp, in a rosy bowl.

Nebular shapes dance, become living things,
And God's presence is felt, in all that man brings.
In this tranquillity, this flow of grace,
In this assessment of the world, and the Human Race.

TOWNELY MEMORIES

"Poor as Lazarus," my mum always said, our good old days were nought, but catch as catch can. People were driven to long dole queues, and the pawn shop. That was if you had anything you could pledge 2/6d being the most you would get, which was just enough to keep body and soul together for another week.

In retrospect, the good old days were my childhood days, bringing back the names of your pals, that were woven into the fabric of your life. There was Rosie, Nora, Ethel too, and Maggie who lived at number 42 Argyle Street in the Whitlefield district, with Padiham via the stepping stones, and Bluebell Wood. One way of getting there was Shanks's Pony, for a piece of happy time. You walked barefoot, with a water bottle, and a package of whatever your cupboard would provide.

One day Billie Lupton, a friend of Ethel's brother Tommy, said, "Why don't we go to Townley Hall next Sunday?"

So we did with happy rapport, making the long walk through the centre of town to Todmorden Road, to the crenel-topped gate-house, that took you over the River Calder, and up along the tree-lined avenue towards Towneley Hall.

The river was a thin trickle of motion, over stones turned to silver, sparkling in welcoming sunshine, which helped our imaginations to work overtime.

Billie told us of a tree carved with a lover's knot and heart. Maggie, now excited wanted to explore the woods, which were so inviting with the clumps of daffodils ready to bud, and shower greenery with golden faces. Each pathway was a challenge to a child's imagination. Billie, was now commanding attention, as he raised a finger to his mouth.

We were about to walk on the first step to the Hall, and looking at one another, each of us said, "This is where a Mr. Ogden, a Curator of long ago, fell through this very step into the gloom of a dungeon, where a skeleton held a piece of parchment in its hand, which disintegrated with the rush of air."

After that six children climbed the remaining steps rather quietly to push open the heavy oak door, and iron handle, to be deposited on the flag-stoned Banquet Hall, where a long oak refrectory table graced its length, with long benches on either side, and chairs on each end, waiting for the banquet to begin. Its well-worn patina was the essence of earlier Elizabethans.

Photos and stag's heads graced the walls and rafters, wrapped up in mystery, and ruby reds and gold's a relief amongst black panelled oak, with slits of sunlight filtering through the open door.

An alabaster figure, nude in stone marble, stood at the bottom of the steps, with an old oak chest under a window donated by some bygone admirer, showing the way to the kitchens, where, bending over a serving hatch we took in the large fireplace and iron spits, and utensils and bowls of long ago. Before moving on we said "Hello" to the great elephant head, planted in the adjacent corner, railed off as steps went down to rooms below, that kept more secrets in the imagination of children's hearts.

Passed a line of lavatories, gained admittance by a penny slot, bar one which was free. I suppose with the likes of us in mind. We would eventually come into a small square room, full of bird cages, where a great black bear stood in a corner, arms raised as if to protect the hundreds of birds of every colour and plumage that sat ready to fly away.

Straight out of the gloom, passages with recessed windows held ancient furniture. On a table, a large bowl decorated in heliographs. It must have been two feet in diameter, it really caught your eye. As did the Queen Anne bed in one of the rooms, where we knew that Queen Elizabeth the First once slept, Along its side stood an old-fashioned oak cradle, on a Persian carpet, with colours that you marvelled at, as you also did at the height of old oak drawers, whose supports were so gnarled away that they seemed ready to revert to the earth from where they grew.

There were small rooms with medals in cases. Valiant heroes were pictured on the walls. Battles won and lost of the India's and Honduras, and the far flung Empire.

Marble busts of Lords and Ladies of Lancashire took their place with the elite of the land. There was ancient pottery and china, their costumes to titivate and wonder at. And the Japanese lady, who with her down-turned eyes, and delicate fan sat demure and shy, in a brilliant wall case, in front of the Taj-Mahal was always a place we wouldn't miss. I still wonder where she went? And the old vestments in cases, before you entered the Chapel, its altar and panels black with age, where we would kneel and say a silent prayer, thinking of King Charles's men, doing the same, when running from Cromwell's men.

Billie would point to a panel and whisper, "A priest's hole, where a tunnel runs out to St. Mary's Church. Messages and secrets. When lives of long ago depended on their passage of time, all in the order of bygone days."

I watched once upon a time six black horses clop clopping down a then cobbled Todmorden Road, their shiny manes blowing in the wind. Sadly O'Hagan's funeral wound its way past the corner of the Wellington Hotel, and St. Mary's Church onto Yorkshire Street, for having fallen out with the Church, she passed on by. "God rest her soul."

So many memories of Towneley Hall, we visited every week, the bubbling rapport which kept us going, subdued and always repressed as we walked her stone-flagged halls. Our whispers really adding to all the wonder of it, just being there, a happy place, where imagination could hold sway, in our home town. A piece of the past, always mine in my heart.

There were mummy cases and Egyptian remains of mummies. A case with its brilliance relieving the sombre tone. The Queen's jewels were so lovely that we all stood and gazed at them for a while, before feasting our eyes on the pictures in the two art galleries, where a seat allowed you time to take in their beauty. So real were they, that you felt that you could just step into the picture into another world, to comfort the lady with teardrops in her eyes.

As time stood still in that so happy time, captured forever all mine! It's not the end, so never mind.

UNEXPECTED PANIC

Observing all, thoughts put into verse,
That registered as clear as a bell,
Of a spate of time in America which I here do tell.
When Ed and Helen made me welcome, with my family as guests,
Allotting us Nancy's room, definitely the best,
Of the children's three for me,
The use of it, I felt a V.I.P.
Now briefly alone my book fell away, I was aware
It was almost the close of day.
As stretched on a lounger, I watched rustling trees sway,
This was eventide, a speedy thing here.
And the colour change in the sky made it pronounced and clear.

With a trepid heart I watched the night come down,
With a stance of trees, now more *en block* I found
Etched more definitely in the darkened sky,
From an apparition of light, suddenly exuding by.
The moon was casting an eerie spell,
Ghosting and shadowing the terrain around.
In its silent glide, through shifting cloud,
And the stillness was singing, growing oppressive and loud.
Vibrating in the woodlands to an ominous note,
To my sensitive ears, in tongues that spoke.
Mysterious, alien, allaying new fears,
Filling my being, palpitating my heart,
As I scanned houses, and patios, remote and apart.

I was alone in a wilderness of unreal time,
In an unknown country, with no one near of mine.
With an impassive moon preening its face,
For its roll into cloud, to emerge with grace

Streaming smugly, its ghostly shine,
In silver shafts, over roofs and shingles of redwood pine.
Hallucinating the moment, circumstances had erringly put me into,
And thrown away the line.
Bolting up now from the lounger
Foregoing my stretched out stance,
White filigree chairs aided the creepy illusion,
With the claw-legged table eager to enhance
This electrical illumination of an ethereal world,
This ghosting of houses, shuttered from the night.
The wind delighting in rattling and abetting the sight,
With fireflies and insects flashing, and winging their way
Into habitats their own, concealed in the day.

The solitude of nature had suddenly turned sour,
My need was for company to alleviate the hour.
Yes I yearned for my relations to banish the gloom,
As swiftly my footsteps carried me inside the room.
Being unfamiliar it was seconds before
I could flick on the light, swish curtains, and lock the sliding door
And unappreciatively settle into luxurious decor
After daring a last peek at the moon once more.

The moon was for lovers, not for a person alone,
With jittery emotions making one a pawn,
To fantasies and things that go bump in the night,
Frightened of their own shadow, and questioning each sound.
Up and down stairs, the house within and around.
I jumped as the phone shrilled, hanging there on the wall,
Saying "Hello" with misgivings, suspicious of the call.
It was for Ed and Helen, I explained, "They wouldn't be long,"
But my voice explained more and they asked what was wrong?
Their concern gave me heart, knowing where to ring a friend,
If help I needed they were there to lend.

At the window now my ears strained for sound
Of a car to break the solitude of the silence around.
God Bless America, a certain song goes,
And I too asked his blessing, as apprehensively I waited
In unwilling repose.
I waited to end this spooky affray,
In my mind, all around
Being nearer the witching hour, than a rational time of the day.
Who said midnight magic, unexpected panic I say.

VICTORIANA

Potted Palms, Aspidistras, horsehair sofas and all
With samplers hung on a scroll-embossed wall.
Chenille curtains with bobs on, ringed on poles
Matching antimacassars worked with small and large holes.
A high mantelshelf, full of photos in frames,
With a roll of honour, in black and gilt names.
Oil lamps on tables covered in plush and lace,
A square marble clock, accurate its pace.
With a monotone tick, with fingers ebony and gold,
Perpetual motion, watching life grow old.
Crisp net curtains shut out the day,
Camouflage for the eye, to rolling hills and the sun's golden ray.
Shutting out visions, and yearnings to fly away
To a Shangrila, to find a timeless day.
From overstuffed rooms, every corner and niche
Caught in a swirl of floating dust, a grand piano denoting the rich
Pampas grass footstools, a chiffonier cluttered there
Complementing a whatnot near a stately winged chair.
Being traditionally upholstered in that prickly horsehair.
Fire irons and a fender in steel and brass, heavily rolled,
The filigree and knobs, kept shining like gold.
A daily nightmare for me the skivvy to bear,
As was the beating of carpets, in the cold morning air.
Not to mention shelves of bric-a-brac, needing handling with care!
In between dreams of miracles to be elsewhere.
Draughty flagged passages had bells on the wall,
Ringing incessantly, to harass an overworked soul
Dead on her feet, doing this, carrying that.

Then to wash and scrub,
With a fire-heated boiler and filled from a cold water tap,
From an old stone sink, near the old dolly tub,
Where hours of drudgery the last crunch
Every Monday morning, till lunch!
A narrow curved stairway
Swept up from the conservatory and hall,
Passed family portraits strewn on the wall
Mingling with plants on pedestals on the floor,
The Aspidistra smothering the stair's bottom, and the door.
Dextrous feet you needed, for treads so steep,
When balancing crockery, it was quite a feat.
Then to relax, or read, in your Spartan room
Was luxury indeed, and a change from wielding mop and broom.
Just a few moments stolen from a jaundice eye,
To feel once more human, time to ask why or why
That this your lot should ever be?
Fettered and harassed, but never free.
For this was a house from a well-worn page
Of a bygone era, dark and gloomy down the age.
Where work was drudgery from dawn to dusk,
And for those with nothing, a way of life - a must!
Where pampered children grew brash without a care,
Expecting, giving orders, with an easy flair.
With no magic carpet to whisk away
The unfortunates slaving, both night and day
In these cluttered rooms, those cheerless halls,
Prisoners in an environment, behind Victorian walls.

WARD 2

The ward was quiet, bathed in golden light,
Good Friday had dawned, ending in a cold night.
The sun now shining had a sham on his face,
No match for the wind, with his blistering pace.
Ward 2 was now brisk, though not many did care,
But the clatter of bedpans was a relief
For those who did dare
To call "Nurse," in a stringent voice,
Elements of nature giving no choice.
Flowers gave colour to lockers bare,
Trollies and windowsills getting more than their share,
Brought by loved ones, who care
For someone there.
The clock on the wall relates only to pain
From weary patients ever watching its frame.
Willing its fingers to sweep the long hours away,
O if only twelve hours did make night and day.
When stuck in hospital, wishing time away.
Nostalgia dripping of hours you never have enough of,
With your partner, with friends, doing the usual stuff.
But that now is for dreams, when leaving Ward 2,
And the overworked nurses, save for the proverbial few
All tarred with the same brush, steady on now, some are good,
Some really care, and don't rush.
For keeping mind and body intact,
Then someday all this will be fiction
Instead of reality, a dead certain fact.
Ward 2 will forever be stuck in your brain,
"We'll meet again," the rapport to the singing of an old refrain.

WHAT COULD IT BE?

Stood on my balcony I took time to stare,
Breathing in the fresh morning air.
Distant woods beckoned the sun,
Inviting through its leaves, tiny prisms of gold
Gilding for fun,
Windows and the now dry eaves.

A sigh of happiness escaped me, it would be a beautiful day,
For to have sun in January, why what else could I say?
The ground rose before me in gentle lines,
Where a well-worn path did twine,
Threading a way through a straddle of elegant pines,
Casually shedding the last of the rain
Into runts along the lane.
A flash of wings filled the sky with a handful of birds,
Whirring by quickly nosing in a tree.
It was a tree that did puzzle me.
It stood well back,
Lower down the track,
Shading an old stone wall its splayed out shape
Like a swinging cape,
Was admired by one and all.
Its green feathery fronds that I could not recall,
Would serve a host of uses, stirring gently in the breeze,
Sylvan and profuse, forming a frieze to please.

Never had I seen such a tree before, it was an intriguing sight,
Growing daily and so much more mysteriously in the night.
I watched it turn lemon, its leaves tinged with gold,
Where tufts into balls had grown.
But it waited the night
And the moon's silver light
To be drenched with mystical dew.
To evolve the last cycle to produce the growth,
That was vital to accumulate the beautiful sight
Of the tree that had held my attention so well,
Had captured my mind, had me under its spell.
Three weeks of my holiday in Spain.
Next morning the sight
That had grown in the night
Solved the puzzle I had pondered in vain.
For the tree swayed proudly all swathed in gold,
It was quite a lovely surprise,
With fluffy showers of feathery balls,
Cradled in every fold.
An exclamation of joy passed my lips,
Ending in a happy sigh.
I should have known what it would be,
As greenery turned yellow to vie
With the blossoms I waited to see,
But unfamiliar, it had me puzzled, and always had eluded me.
Yes you have guessed it, have got it right,
This lovely gorgeous sight,
Was a newly-blossomed golden mimosa tree.

WHAT WILL MY QUEEN BE DOING TODAY?

I must write to my Queen, it is the only way to lift my heart and temper today. My clothes I have finished, the ashes are emptied, I have replenished the fire, dusted the dust into an obscure pyre.

The kitchen dishes are stacked and draining, now await the next call for sustenance, none repetition miraculous, thoughts fleeting and waning. Doing nothing to inspire any culinary desire, for alas and alack my taste-buds are zeros, and well pushed back. Thus the reason for thoughts on a higher plain, having nothing to lose, and nothing to gain.

Be that as it may I must go on to say, "What will my Queen be doing today? Are her corridors and rooms all dusted and groomed, and brightened with roses to complement her moods? Do her draining boards hold, china galore, with motifs agleam, and fit for a Queen? I would be scared to drop them on the floor. Old-fashioned or modern her kitchen will hold efficient hands, producing hot or cold succulent tit-bits and tempting bites, where baking and grilling waft savoury thoughts, releasing my taste-buds in a longing delight."

I sometimes bought a relished dream from A to B, from her to me, a happy sojourn you could say, revelry and fantasy very ofey. For a short while mundane things had melted away. For lovely thoughts, like dreams, effect one that way. So in this dalliance so tempting, awhile I will stay, all beautiful and gay, no not in that way!

But just saying again and again, in a wondering way, "What will my Queen be doing today?"

WINTER

An icy gown of snow and hail,
Scattered the immediate hill and dale,
Giving the world a hint, a gleam,
Of winter wrath, her freezing spleen.
Snubbing the earth in her soft green bed,
Of an Indian summer, so cunningly led
Into the throes of a November day,
Shattering with the fury of a scathing wind.
Claiming winter status, the sun to rescind.
Winter had surely staked her claim,
Drab and grey the leadened sky
Showing Nature the time, the moment was now
To dress in accord and take a bow
Out of the sun that had boasted its pride,
Gilding the trees in their autumn gown.
Bringing people flocking, from their nearby town.
To revel in the glory of late summer days,
An Indian summer, now quick to change her ways.
To give into the last of the seasonal flow,
With winter the master, all cold and aglow
With the power of the North wind on his side,
With the polar regions, abating with pride
Just giving a forecast of what lies in store.
Fog, ice and snow,
Blustering wind and rain
Oh for the spring and the summer again!

WINTER AGAIN

Winter flaunts her special art,
Engraving town and park.
Nothing too complex in her cold pass by,
Chilly fingers pointing, reaching high,
Reaching low,
Her freezing wind abetting so.
Cascading waters, fluid flow,
Stalagmited down below.
No bird can sip
This solid drip.
Grassy verges stiffened white,
Black veined trees, a ghostly sight.
Phantom sentinels in repose,
With red brick walls paling sickly, as the night does close.
In zero ratings now in swing,
No man or beast escapes its sting.
The air we breathe, puffed out white,
Faces pinched, noses red, vermilion fingers clenched up tight.
Daunting this traveller from outer space,
This frozen intruder confusing the pace
Of the daily round
Of winter vagaries, speculation rife to the unpredictable sound
Of drip, drip, drip, at last the thaw,
What comes next, will it be the snow?

WISHES

If only was the theme we discussed down the years,
Wishing for this, wishing for that,
It sort of helped our dreams and schemes roll off pat.
Strands of life that somehow went astray
Mixed with memories of a far off day.
How I wish things had turned out a certain way.
I had wished for the moon, one person's view,
All my wishes related, and always for two.
I had it planned up there on cloud nine,
All my wishes fulfilled, everything fine!
Fantasies creeping, dreaming away,
Secret wishes, bursting each day.
Locked in your soul, your heart full of all the happiness derived
From all the wishes contrived
In the moonlight's magic, in the miracles of the night
When you floated in dreams, all wishes turning in sight.
Pensively I sigh in a new dawning day,
Wishing to capture the dream, that had floated away.
Do wishes come true, well maybe a few, maybe some do.
Wishes, like dreams, are life's gifts, always on cue.

WORDS

Words the forte for the human race,
Strategically placed, showing the pace.
Words of conflict, a coiling rope
Of fear, of anxiety, without a fraction of hope.
Words of enchantment depict a beautiful scene,
With a cadence of clarity, luminous clean.
Words of kindness, warmth to a lonely soul,
Banish the solitude knell, show a brighter goal.
Words, menacing, fractious, growing strong,
Booming in hatred the warning gong.
Words of arrogance challenging all,
Fanatics head the boasting call.
Words so tender, sensuous, warm,
A soothing legato, a healing balm.
Words of wisdom, quick to disperse
In the oily flow of a traitor's curse.
Words so innocent, from the lips of a child,
Laughter ensuing happy and mild.
Words spoke in all tongues, the intent the same,
With words of love, of hate, and the power game.
Words of prayer, of thanks whispered low,
Worded in rosary, sincerely so!
Words of a plea, a desperate call,
Embracing Mankind, without inhibition or gall.
Words of tolerance, to other's actions unkind,
To understanding and compassion, in the ultimate find.
Words reaching out, simple to learn,
To a heart and soul for forgiveness, which how many do yearn?
Words of greeting ringing true,
Exuding pleasure from me to you.
Words of hope, soothing a soul's decline,
Let them be remembered, both yours and mine!

WORDS FROM A KIND PERSON

A few years ago, I was coming from Church when I bumped into an old friend on Brunshaw Avenue. We both had lived on Anne Street when all the old terraced houses were up. Her mother-in-law had once had one of those 'everything shops' at the end, cornering onto Higgins Street, that were in those days lifesavers for the poor families.

It was Mary Riley, and what she said to me that Sunday morning comes back to me yet when I am feeling down and depressed. It suddenly slips out from the recesses of my mind, and somehow gives me a bit of comfort.

"I read in the paper of Herbert's death a few weeks ago," she said then.

I nodded thinking about my late husband, and Mary went on.

"You must know how sorry I am. His mother and sister Eva, they were such good friends and customers."

The last two words were spoken with a semblance of a smile. More words followed with me just standing there listening.

"You know it is twelve months since I lost my Alf. And as you do, I had always said to those bereaved how sorry I was. But until it happened to me, the words were taken for granted. Then I vowed that I would never say them again to anyone, but here I am again doing just that."

Still I stood there listening to Mary's next words, when I noticed tears had filled her eyes.

"You see," she continued, "I was mopping my front doorstep after Alf died, and I thought to myself. Why am I doing this when there is no one to note if it is clean or not? There is no one to know your heartache as they say, so sorry!"

Feeling rather bewildered, I can't remember exactly what I replied, but I knew that she understood a person's loss and sorrow when your partner is taken away from you. I was trying to explain how words are sometimes so inadequate, yet a kind word can be worth more than all the world.

Then quietly in my mind I spoke the names of all the old friendly neighbours who had lived on Anne Street. It mounted to a lot of names, and being three blocks long it took me quite some time.

I said, "God Rest their Souls."

The old days were hard, but somehow you felt more happy and content, for you always felt that you somehow belonged to that caring band of people.

YESTERYEARS

Yesteryears, the mould fashioned a billion lives,
Broke so many hearts on the great divide.
The treadmill was a carousel, when feet stepped light
Into a future of youth, advancing into the night.

You and I, were puppets on a revolving stage,
Playing at living, thinking we knew each page
In the book of life, so comparatively new,
Flicked through with indifference, with a personal view.

Inevitable involvement coming with each new dawn,
Humanity embracing, where love was born.
The years, no consequence, life was for today,
Crowding, pushing in our own special way.

The orbit halcyon, the soul is light,
The hearts beat in colour, in a jewel-bright night.
Far away places, a dream in the eye,
With old and new loves, one quite special, taking you high.

Roots prone to wander, gathering strength on the way,
Twine with tautening threads, the nostalgic back-cloth for another day
The past aura of yesteryears, forgotten until,
Voices vibrate the silence, in a room so still.

Years left behind, leap in happy recall,
Unleashing memories, that gently fall
From glorious youth, with the sun on your back
Inhibitions free, with the partner fate decided,
Would be your own knave, your own special Jack.

Helped over the stile, you splash through the mud,
Together the tallest bluebells, in the heart of the wood.
A piece of tapestry, this pattern of life,
Coloured with happiness, and shaded with strife.

Humanity resilient, laughter and song,
Brought a whole lot of loving, carrying you along.
Lingering in the aura of past reminisce
The silence so beautiful bending the will,
So full of desire, so filled with voices,
Now forever still!

YOUR LONELY ROOM

Alone in your room it gets harder to bear, and you sometimes imagine that someone is there. But the only sound, is the fall of the rain, as it pours from the broken eaves. Even the birds are silent now, flying for shelter into the trees.

Then an angry wind blusters and blows, bending, swaying, and rustling the leaves, bringing fluttering flows of startled birds, twittering around, hastily scratching and pecking the ground, only to fly off again to a drier niche, to a broken drain in a nearby ditch. These are mundane things to the passer-by, who steps out briskly with a determined gait, to get up and do for her immediate few.

You rate a stare, and a quick wonder why do you stand at your window as she goes by? But each to his or her own, as they say, her thoughts aren't for you, they are far away, you are simply a lone figure along their way.

Then the drone of a plane you hear in the sky, and you say a prayer in your mind as it fades to die, for it is something foreign to your concept, to fly on high somewhere near the moon, miles and miles from your lonely room. Still patiently watching in the oncoming gloom, for a glimpse of anything, anywhere, outside your room, outside the confines of your windowpane, that can break the silence that is stagnating your brain.

A few minutes more, then you heave a sigh, for you have seen the last of the passers by; so you turn from the view of the trees in the lane, and the end of the gable glistening like steel, swimming with rivulets of sheeting rain. You swish the curtains to blot out the sight, then reach with tense fingers to flick on the light.

Your thoughts still fluid, rock to and fro, you explore new television channels, and wonder how things will go, as you do your last chore, in the usual way. You muse on tomorrow, and plan a new day.

To push back the shadows that crowd in your head, you think, indeed you just have to think of new things to do, for anything would be better than the plight that is you. And so you continue, with a make-believe game, of practical schemes that somehow take a false trail, turning to fantasy in a web of dreams.

Well maybe tomorrow will be a sunshiny day, for you have got the feeling that someone new is coming your way, and inviting you out to mix and stray into the world of people, who will dispel your gloom, and dismiss the quietness of your lonely room.